Dreams and Visions

Kurt Bangert

Dreams and Visions

An Autobiographical Journey Across Five Continents

© 2026 Kurt Bangert
Dreams and Visions
An Autobiographical Journey Across Five Continents
www.kurtbangert.de

Bibliographic Information of the German National Library:
The German National Library lists this publication in the
German National Bibliography. Detailed bibliographic data can be
accessed online at: dnb.dnb.de.

Editing, typesetting und design:
Philia, Bad Nauheim

Publisher:
BoD · Books on Demand GmbH,
Überseering 33, 22297 Hamburg,
bod@bod.de

Print: Libri Plureos GmbH,
Friedensallee 273, 22763 Hamburg

Cover Picture:
Kurt Bangert

ISBN: 978-3-7693-1548-6

I dedicate this book to Aline
with whom I shared a very substantial portion
of my life

Content

Preface

This book is a journey through memory—woven from the land-scapes I've walked, the people I've met, and the quiet transfor-mations that shaped me along the way. I never set out to collect stories for their own sake, but over the years, life offered more than I could hold in silence: fragments of joy, loss, tragedy, awe, and learning that quietly asked to be remembered.

Having traveled across five continents, lived among vast-ly different cultures, and shared moments with people from all walks of life, I've come to see that what unites us often lies beneath the surface. Through these pages, I hope not only to recount events, but to reflect on the deeper threads—of connec-tion, wonder, resilience, and the unexpected grace that some-times meets us in the most unlikely places.

This is not a complete record—nor could it be. Memory is a living thing, shaped as much by time as by geography. What you will find here is simply my own truth, told as faithfully as I can recall it, with gratitude for all that has been given, and all that has been endured.

If there is a purpose to these pages, it is not to instruct, but to share—something of the journey, and perhaps, something of the soul behind it.

Kurt Bangert

Early Years

As a young boy, I had been a rather quiet soul—at least, that was how I saw myself. An introvert. A boy of few words. I had never been one to gather many friends around me. Prior to going to school, there had been one short friendship with a boy from the neighborhood, but he was never a close companion. In time, even his name faded from my memory.

At elementary school, solitude became my shadow. Yet solitude was not always a burden. Often, it felt like home. It wrapped around me like a familiar cloak, shielding me from the unspoken.

My parents were loving in their way—caring, dutiful—but they had never been taught the language of emotions, let alone their intrinsic value. In their household, feelings were unwelcome guests, acknowledged only to be dismissed. If my mother, my older brother Bernd, or I myself ever dared to speak of sorrow or unease, our father's response was swift and resolute: "You don't have to feel that way." And so, we learned not to. Emotions were neither discussed nor examined; they were something to be avoided, ignored, erased. It was a legacy of the post-war times.

The war had ended not long before, but its shadow lingered. Our parents had emerged from its horrors, not unscathed but hardened. Our mother had lived through relentless bombardments, explosions tearing through the air, some perilously close. She had survived, outwardly untouched—lovely still, but quiet, timid. Our father had fought on both the French and Russian fronts, enduring the brutality of winters that swallowed men whole. (Image: Paul Bangert as Soldier)

In one bitter season, a Russian sharpshooter had nearly claimed his life. The bullet tore through one cheek and exited the other, shattering most of his lower teeth. He remembered thinking, with eerie admiration, "That was a perfect shot." He was carried on a skeletal stretcher to a hospital, slipping between life and death, but he survived. And in the German army, survival meant submission—to duty, to command, to the unflinching suppression of fear. Emotion had no place in war. Nor, it seemed, in the home our father built afterward.

My father often spoke of his war years, his stories orbiting, again and again, around his time in Russia. The brutal winters, the endless marches, the near brushes with death. Leave was a rare luxury, and when granted, it never seemed enough. More than once, he overstayed his permitted days, choosing stolen moments of respite over duty—only to find himself imprisoned upon return.

Yet for all his service, he harbored no admiration for the man who had sent him to war. He despised Hitler—his ruthless militarism, his deceit, his intoxicating populism. To him, the *Führer* was a destroyer, not a savior. But our mother had seen a different side. To her, Hitler had been the leader who lifted Germany from the depths of the Great Depression, who had given the nation back its pride. In our household, the past was not just history—it was a fault line, running quietly beneath our lives.

My mother was a quiet soul with whom I deeply resonated. She was caring, loving, and self-sacrificing—often putting others before herself. Though at times emotional, her heart was always in the right

place. A woman of deep faith, she remained steadfast in her religious values and lived them with quiet conviction. (Image previous page: Else Bangert)

Both parents had endured harrowing times and, when the war finally ended, their greatest relief was simply being alive. They had married in the midst of the chaos, in 1942. My brother Bernd was born in early 1944; I saw the light of day in July 1946—a child of the fragile peace that followed the storm. (Image: Kurt and Bernd)

The post-war years were marked by hardship, by hunger, by an ever-present uncertainty about what the future might hold. Yet, compared to the war, they felt almost merciful. At least now, survival did not depend on the whim of bombs or the cruelty of the front. And with Hitler gone, there was a sense—perhaps fragile, but real—that things could only improve from now on.

Photographs from those early years tell the story without words. In the grainy black-and-white images, our parents appear gaunt, their faces drawn, their bodies thinned by years of deprivation. And yet, beside them, the two boys stand sturdy and well-fed. It was no accident. Our parents had made a silent, unwavering decision: Their children would not know hunger, not as they had. And so, while the boys ate their fill, mother and father scraped by on what little remained, wearing their sacrifices as quietly as they wore their tattered post-war clothes. (Image: Mother, Kurt, Father, Bernd)

My brother and I were, for the most part, well-behaved. But there was one incident—so vivid, so unforgettable—that it seared itself into our memories like an old scar.

It happened on a visit to a grandaunt's rural home, somewhere on the outskirts of Mönchengladbach. The visit itself faded into obscurity, but this moment remained: While our parents lingered in conversation with the elderly woman, we both, weary from being patient listeners, wandered outside, eager to leave.

Near the house, we discovered a gaping, square hole in the ground, brimming with foul-smelling manure—a cesspool of rot and filth. Being about five years old at the time, I stood at its edge, staring into the bubbling muck, wrinkling my nose at the stench, when I sensed movement behind me. Turning, I met my brother Bernd's smirking face, approaching me in silence.

I stepped aside, granting Bernd a clearer view of the pit. My brother peered in, curiosity replacing amusement as he studied the wretched mire. And then, with deliberate slowness, I took a step forward.

And pushed.

It was the gentlest of nudges, just enough to tip the balance.

Bernd toppled forward, flailing, but managed—just barely—to throw out his arms at the last moment, gripping the edges of the pit. The rest of him, however, was not so lucky. From the neck down, he was submerged in the thick, reeking sludge, only his shocked, spluttering face visible above the filth.

Hearing the commotion, our parents rushed outside to find Bernd, wide-eyed and sputtering, half-submerged in the murky filth. The farewell was forgotten; the visit, unintentionally prolonged. Clothes had to be washed, the shivering boy scrubbed clean, and then came the wait—for fabric to dry, for tempers to cool.

While Bernd endured the aftermath of his muddy ordeal, I found myself led away by my father, through the garden and out of sight. Father stopped, turned to me, and asked a simple question:

"Do you deserve punishment?"

Without hesitation, I admitted that I did.

A "good beating" followed. Corporal punishment was not only common in those days but considered a parental duty, a necessity for raising decent men. Father would often invoke Scripture, citing Proverbs 13:24: "He that spareth his rod hateth his son: but he that loveth him chasteneth him."

A cane rested permanently atop the kitchen cabinet, always within reach, its mere presence a silent warning. Whether it was ever used on me, I cannot say with absolute certainty. More often than not, the threat was enough—a single wave of the cane, a sharp look, and mischief was abandoned.

My brother, however, was less fortunate. Bernd received his share of punishments, while I, quick-witted and nimble at times, found ways to slip free. I seemed to have a gift—one my father secretly admired. With a well-timed remark, a clever turn of phrase, I could make father laugh, and his laughter, more often than not, was my escape. Perhaps that was why, despite everything, I remained father's favorite.

Our parents were devout members of the conservative Seventh-day Adventist Church, a faith that set them apart in ways both subtle and profound. Unlike most people around us, who observed Sunday as the Lord's Day, Adventists worshipped on Saturday—the Old Testament Sabbath. This distinction was more than a matter of scheduling; it was a conviction rooted in the belief that the Bible was the inerrant Word of God, to be interpreted literally and obeyed to the letter.

For Bernd and myself, this faith came at a cost. In those days, German schools still held classes on Saturdays, but our parents forbade us from attending. Instead, while our classmates sat at their desks, we were in church, listening to sermons, singing hymns, and marking ourselves as different. Our absence made us outsiders, setting us apart in a way that neither of us welcomed.

The practical consequences were just as burdensome. Each Monday, we returned to school having missed an entire day of lessons, forced to rely on classmates to relay assignments—an arrangement that was unreliable at best. Sometimes, the messages were incomplete; other times, they never arrived at all. And so, there were Mondays when we faced our teachers empty-handed, our unfinished homework a silent testimony to the faith that governed our lives.

Although a Catholic school was just around the corner, our parents chose instead to send their boys to a Lutheran elementary school farther away. Each morning, we walked the mile-long journey, passing through streets still scarred by war. The bombings of September 1944 had left much of the area in ruins—houses reduced to rubble, blackened skeletons of buildings standing as silent witnesses to past devastation. But to me, this wasteland of shattered stone and ash was unremarkable. It was simply the world as I had always known it.

After four years of elementary school, I advanced to middle school—a small but significant step. There was no tradition of higher education in our family; neither of our parents had attended *Gymnasium*, the rigorous academic high school that led to university. They came from working-class backgrounds, where ambition stretched only as far as securing steady employment.

At middle school, I found a friend in Erwin, the son of a stationery shop owner. But academically, I was unremarkable. My grades hovered between B's, C's, and the occasional D—mediocre by any standard. One day, my class teacher summoned my father for a private conversation. The message was blunt: "With his intelligence, Kurt should be earning only top marks," my teacher told Dad. But intelligence alone was not enough.

No amount of admonition could change what lay at the heart of the matter: I lacked drive. I was neither ambitious nor diligent. Preparing for lessons was a task I postponed until it was too late, if I bothered at all. My mind was elsewhere, lost in daydreams, wandering through thoughts that had little to do with my schoolwork. I was no go-getter, not a hard worker—just a boy more inclined to muse than to strive.

Our family lived in a modest three-room flat on the fourth floor of a four-storey corner house at Bozener Straße 34 in Mönchengladbach. Calling it an "apartment" would have been a stretch—there was no proper entrance door separating our living space from the staircase, no designated kitchen, and no bathroom. A small sink was by the landing, and the only toilet—a cramped, windowless cubicle—was two floors down.

At the time, Mönchengladbach was little more than a name on a map, unknown beyond its own region. Only years later would it rise to fame, carried into European recognition by its legendary soccer team, winners of two continental trophies.

One day, without much preamble, our father made an announcement: we were moving. Not just to another street or another neighborhood, but to an entirely different region—and to a better apartment, he assured us.

For me, it was a farewell to the only world I had known. I would leave behind my school friends, our church community, the familiar streets of my childhood. And yet, the prospect of the unknown held its own thrill. A new environment, a new home—change was unsettling, but it also shimmered with possibility.

In the Country Side

Our family's new home lay within the sprawling grounds of *Gut Arienheller*, a baron's estate near Rheinbrohl, on the edge of the *Westerwald*—a breath-taking expanse of rolling hills, dense forests, and sun-dappled meadows, where orchards spilled over with fruit and the Rhine flowed not far beyond. It was a world apart from the gray streets of Mönchengladbach, a place where nature stretched in every direction, untamed and full of quiet beauty.

The move had come about swiftly. A friend and colleague of my father had mentioned an empty flat on the estate, and the decision was made almost at once. The baron and his family occupied the ground floor, while the friend's family and my family took up residence on the upper level, now sharing not just a home, but a daily life.

Both families had two sons, though I and my brother were slightly older than our new neighbors. The boys quickly became playmates, their lives intertwined through shared adventures and the simple joys of being young. Beyond the home, our bond extended to the church pews, as both families worshipped together, bound by faith and friendship in equal measure.

The baron presided over a vast estate, a world unto itself, where fields had to be sown and harvested, forests tended, and livestock cared for. The farm bustled with life—cows, pigs, chickens, and geese roamed the grounds, while dogs and cats kept watch over the land. Fresh milk was available straight from the cow's udder, still warm and frothy, a simple luxury that city life had never offered.

My mother was given a small garden of her own, a patch of earth where she cultivated peas, tomatoes, and other vegetables. Occasionally, I was called upon to help—pulling weeds, watering the plants—but my enthusiasm for such tasks was fleeting. My limbs grew sluggish, my hands heavy with the monotony of farmwork. It was not a labor I enjoyed.

Yet, in spite of that, country life was a revelation. The air was fresher, the days quieter, and the nearness of nature brought a sense of wonder. Here, beneath open skies and among the whispering trees, I felt something I had never quite grasped before—a closeness to God.

I had been raised in faith, taught to sit still in church, to listen, to obey, to believe in the Bible. Even before going to school, I had vowed to myself that as soon as I learned to read and write, I would read the entire Bible from cover to cover. Religion to me was what one would believe about the Bible, about God, about God's creation, about how to be saved. But now, divinity seemed not only confined to sermons and scripture but present in the rustling of leaves, in the vastness of the fields, in the golden light of dusk.

To attend middle school, I now faced a daily journey that tested both my endurance and my sense of belonging. Each morning, I had to walk several miles to Bad Hönningen, where I boarded a train for an half-hour ride to Neuwied, and then walked another ten minutes to reach my new school. There, as a newcomer, I again felt like an outsider. My grades remained unremarkable, yet I persevered and managed to complete middle school.

Not long after, I began an apprenticeship as a typesetter at a large printing house in Neuwied. For the next three years, my routine remained unchanged—commuting back and forth between Rheinbrohl and the city, caught between two worlds.

Outside of work, I would spent time in the Baron's fields but also playing soccer with friends; but my greatest joy came from playing table tennis with Andreas, the older son of our neighbors. The two of us could spend hours at the table, exchanging rapid volleys, pausing only to catch our breath and talk a bit.

Life in the countryside had been unlike anything we had known before— vast, open, full of new experiences. It was nothing like the war-scarred streets of Mönchengladbach. The rolling hills, the camaraderie, the endless games of table tennis—all of it had given me a new sense of belonging. But as with all chapters in life, this one, too, came to an end.

At first, it was Andreas's family who left, moving to Hamburg. Not long after, our own family relocated to Berlin, and just like that, the friendship that had seemed so central to daily life faded into the past. For decades, our paths never crossed.

Andreas, never one for religious devotion, pursued a career in acting before eventually finding his niche in product placement. I, meanwhile, took a different route, one that would later lead me to work as a PR Director and press spokesman for a relief agency.

More than forty years passed before both of our names resurfaced in each other's lives—I came across an article about Andreas in the media, while Andreas stumbled upon my name in a newspaper. The past, long buried, suddenly felt within reach. Curious and nostalgic, I picked up the phone and called my old friend. I offered to visit him, and Andreas welcomed the idea. When we finally met again after four decades, the first words Andreas spoke were unexpected:

"You were the one who taught me how to think", he said to me, as if this was a matter of course.

The admission took me by surprise—and filled me with quiet joy. It was a reminder that the impact we have on others, whether great or small, is often invisible to us. Influence, like memory, lingers in ways we may never fully grasp. I was reminded of a quote from Albert Schweitzer:

"Not one of us knows what effect his life produces, and what he gives to others; that is hidden from us and must remain so, though we are sometimes allowed to see some little fraction of it, so that we may not lose courage. The way in which power works is a mystery."

Discovering Berlin

But let me return to the time when we moved from Rheinbrohl to Berlin. Sometime in 1965, my father received a phone call in which he was offered a position with the Adventist Church in Berlin. Without hesitation, he accepted, and soon the family was preparing for yet another move—this time, to a city unlike I had ever known.

Berlin was no ordinary place. Though politically part of West Germany, it was geographically stranded within the borders of East Germany, an island of the West encircled by the East. The scars of war still marked the city, both physically and politically.

To understand Berlin's unique situation, one has to look back to the final days of World War II. When Nazi Germany surrendered in May 1945, the victorious Allies—the United States, the United Kingdom, France, and the Soviet Union—divided Germany into four occupation zones. Berlin, as the former capital, was likewise split into four sectors, each controlled by one of the occupying powers.

However, as tensions between East and West escalated, the division of Germany became permanent. In May 1949, the three Western zones united under a new constitution to form the *Federal Republic of Germany*—better known as *West Germany*. In response, the Soviet-controlled zone was transformed into the *German Democratic Republic*, or *East Germany*.

Berlin also became a divided city. The three Western sectors—controlled by the U.S., the U.K. and France—became known collectively as *West Berlin*, while the Soviet-controlled sector was absorbed into East Germany and declared its capital. Thus, West Berlin became an isolated enclave of democracy, completely surrounded by East Germany, a city cut off from its own hinterland by a ring of checkpoints, barbed wire, and watchtowers. For me, the move to Berlin was not just a geographical shift—it was an immersion into the heart of the Cold War, a city where history itself seemed to hang in the air.

East Germany was more than just a neighboring state—it was a tightly controlled Communist regime, firmly under Soviet influence. Along with Poland, Czechoslovakia, Hungary, Romania, and Bulgaria, it was one of the Soviet Union's many satellite states, each ruled by a government that answered not to its own people, but to Moscow's will.

By 1952, the German Democratic Republic (GDR or "East Germany") had reinforced its borders with the West, erecting a fortified demarcation line to prevent East Germans from fleeing to freedom. Legal crossings were granted only under strict conditions, effectively sealing off an entire population from the Western world.

Tensions erupted on June 17, 1953, when years of economic hardship and political repression triggered a mass uprising across East Germany. Thousands of workers took to the streets, demanding better wages, free elections, and an end to Soviet rule. For a brief moment, it seemed as though the Communist government might fall. But the rebellion was swiftly and brutally crushed—Soviet tanks rolled into the streets, opening fire on protesters, restoring order through sheer force.

In the West, the memory of that failed uprising lived on. West Germany declared June 17 a national holiday, a tribute to the courage of those who had stood against tyranny. In East Germany, however, the mere mention of that day was met with silence—or worse, repression. The scars of that moment remained an unspoken reminder of the iron grip that held the country in place.

Berlin had become the last escape hatch for East Germans yearning for freedom. While the rest of the border between East and West Germany had been heavily fortified, the internal division of Berlin remained relatively open—at least for a time. Thousands seized the opportunity to cross from East to West, with numbers surging alarmingly in 1961. That year alone, more than 8,000 people fled, among them doctors, engineers, intellectuals, and skilled workers—those whose absence threatened the stability of the East German economy.

Faced with this escalating brain drain, the East German government, with full Soviet backing, took drastic action. On August 13, 1961, in the dead of night, construction began on what would become one of the most infamous symbols of the Cold War: the *Berlin Wall*. Soldiers and workers rolled out barbed wire barriers, later replaced with towering concrete slabs. Streets were torn apart, train lines severed, families and friends abruptly and permanently divided. What had once been an invisible line became an impenetrable fortress, slicing the city in two. The Berlin Wall loomed as a stark symbol of a divided city, cutting through streets, neighborhoods, even families.

From that moment on, escape became virtually impossible. Only a privileged few—high-ranking officials, trusted party members, and select government-approved travelers—were granted exit permits. For the ordinary East German citizen, the world beyond the wall was now forever out of reach.

But despite the danger, some still dared to defy the regime. Ingenious escape attempts ranged from tunneling beneath the wall to soaring over it in homemade hot-air balloons. Others braved the perilous crossing disguised as diplomats, hidden in car trunks, or even swimming across treacherous waterways. But for every successful escape, many others failed. The *death strip*, a barren, heavily guarded zone flanking the wall, became a graveyard for those caught in the act. More than 300 people were shot or otherwise killed in their desperate bid for freedom.

The Berlin Wall stood as a chilling testament to the stark divide between oppression and liberty, a concrete embodiment of the Cold War's unforgiving realities. For nearly three decades, it would remain an unyielding barrier.

For Westerners traveling from West Germany to West Berlin, the journey was anything but straightforward. Since West Berlin was an isolated enclave surrounded by East Germany, reaching it required crossing through Communist-controlled territory—either by train or by car. This *transit travel* was strictly regulated, and every trip was a test of patience.

At the East German border, travelers were met by stone-faced border guards, notorious for their meticulous inspections and deliberate intimidation tactics. Every passport was scrutinized, every face compared to its photograph with an air of suspicion. Vehicles were thoroughly searched—trunks popped open, suitcases unzipped, and even car seats sometimes probed for hidden compartments. The process could take minutes or drag on for hours, depending on the whims of the guards. At times, they seemed to delay travelers just for the sake of harassment. Once cleared, travelers had to remain on the designated transit Autobahn, forbidden from exiting or making detours into East German territory. Straying from the route was not just discouraged—it was illegal and could lead to arrest.

Unlike transit travel, officially visiting East Germany required a visa, which was not granted lightly. Only those with legitimate reasons—such as visiting relatives—stood a chance of obtaining one. But for me and my family, there was no compelling reason to visit the East. We had no family there, and the allure of Communist East Germany was nonexistent. To us, it was a bleak, joyless place, devoid of the vibrancy and freedom we cherished in the West.

12

By contrast, West Berlin was a dazzling metropolis, brimming with life, energy, and culture. It stood in stark contrast to the drab austerity of East Berlin, which seemed frozen in time. The heart of the city was the *Kurfürstendamm*—a grand boulevard lined with elegant department stores, chic boutiques, bustling cafés, and neon-lit cinemas. Here, I discovered a world of entertainment and sophistication unlike anything I had known before.

Having spent the last five years in the quiet countryside, I was captivated by the sheer excitement of city life. The lights, the music, the people—it all felt like a gateway to something bigger. The legendary "Berliner Luft" ("Berlin air") was more than just a phrase; it embodied the city's spirit of freedom, creativity, and boundless possibility. The famous 1904 song by Paul Lincke, titled "Berliner Luft," had long been an anthem of the city's exuberance, still played today as a favorite encore by the Berlin Philharmonic Orchestra at the annual open-air summer concert, when audiences would enthusiastically clap along, celebrating the unmistakable rhythm of Berlin itself.

For me, Berlin was more than a new home—it was the threshold of a new life, a world away from the rural simplicity of Rheinbrohl. Here, I could breathe in the intoxicating promise of the modern world, a place where anything seemed possible.

Having completed my apprenticeship as a compositor in Neuwied, it was now time for me to find a job. As a typesetter in an era before computers, the job was grueling. Much of the day was spent standing at a letter case, meticulously placing each lead letter into a composing stick. In Berlin, I worked at several different printing houses, but none of them felt quite right. The 8-hour workdays felt monotonous, and the constant standing soon wore me down.

Those years were also a time of great technological change in the printing industry, and I could feel the winds of transformation blowing. Few professions would evolve so radically in the coming years as typesetting. Soon, photocomposition emerged, and while it was initially seen as a progressive shift, I never found myself drawn to it. The technology seemed cumbersome to me, lacking the tactile artistry of manual typesetting.

However, as the decades wore on, and computers began to reshape the world, I grew more intrigued by the rise of desktop publishing. This new wave of technology not only allowed for the digital creation and layout of printed material but also empowered individuals to write and design books themselves. Later in life, I would find the idea of creating and publishing my own works exciting. But back in the late Sixties, in Berlin, I knew this was not the work I would spend the rest of my life doing. The job was a stepping stone, and the pull of something greater, something more aligned with my own aspirations, was beginning to take shape. I began going to school again – in the evening, trying to finish secondary education and hoping to study at a university. But I did not quite finish the school – due to an unexpected turn of events that would change the direction of my life once again.

The American Dream

Already at an early age, I had been captivated by a film about the United States, and ever since, I dreamed of visiting that land of endless possibilities. My fascination only deepened when, from time to time, Americans would visit our church. As a conservative Christian, I found myself drawn to the influence these visitors had, and I began to feel a connection to a world far beyond my own.

My curiosity for the U.S. was further piqued when I attended an evangelistic campaign by the American preacher Billy Graham, whose powerful presence and message left a lasting impression on me. In the Sixties, the U.S. was still a beacon of hope and opportunity for many Germans. After all, it was the U.S. that had liberated Germany from the brutal grip of a dictator who had plunged us into another devastating World War. That war not only ended in a crushing defeat but also split Germany into two hostile states, a division that would last for four long decades. For many of us Germans, the United States of America were seen not just as liberators but as symbols of freedom, progress, and new beginnings.

Like so many others, I viewed the U.S. as a land where anything seemed possible, a place where dreams could be realized. The notion of visiting this country, experiencing its vast landscapes, its modern culture, and its boundless opportunities, became an aspiration that would shape my future ambitions.

One day, while attending a religious conference in Vienna, I met a charming young lady from Tennessee. The connection between us was immediate, and we began a lively correspondence that soon blossomed into something more. This exchange of letters marked the beginning of a new chapter in my life.

Fueled by my dream of experiencing the land of endless possibilities, I made the bold decision to leave Germany behind. In 1968, I set off on my first great adventure, traveling with Icelandic Airlines. My journey took me via Reykjavik to New York, then on to Chicago, before finally arriving in Nashville, Tennessee.

It was a transformative journey. The sights, the sounds, the vastness of America—it was a world I had only read about or seen in films, but now I was living it. Little did I know, this trip would not only fulfill a dream but would alter the course of my life forever. The experiences, challenges, and opportunities awaiting me in the United States would shape my future in ways I could never have imagined.

In Nashville, I had the opportunity to meet Gerhard Hasel, a German Adventist who had immigrated to the U.S. to pursue theological studies. Gerhard was nearing the completion of his PhD at Vanderbilt University and would go on to become one of the most well-known Adventist theologians, eventually teaching at the Adventist Theological Seminary of Andrews University in Berrien Springs, Michigan.

During one of our conversations, Gerhard offered me an intriguing perspective on his thinking. Reflecting on his time at the university, he mused:

"My non-Adventist teachers at Vanderbilt all have their predisposed assumptions and practice historical criticism without questioning its validity," he said. "So I have decided, with equal certainty, to abide by my evangelical, Biblical presuppositions, and not question them."

This approach made it possible for Gerhard to reconcile his Adventist beliefs with academic theology, allowing him to maintain a conservative, literal interpretation of the Bible while avoiding internal conflict with modern theological ideas. He encouraged me to adopt a similar approach.

But being deeply committed to seeking truth above all else, I was skeptical. I thought to myself, "I will certainly not follow Gerhard's advice and accept any presuppositions without thoroughly investigating them. I am here to ask questions. I am here to search for truth." I resolved to study theology in order to learn the truth. Truth to me became more important than orthodoxy.

Gerhard had found comfort in certainty, while I was determined to embrace the journey of questioning and exploration, even if it meant challenging long-held assumptions and cherished beliefs. This willingness to question and search for deeper understanding would guide me throughout my life and studies.

On a completely different note, while in Nashville, I became acquainted with country music, a genre that was initially not to my liking. The type of

country music I saw and heard on local TV struck me as a cultural peculiarity, something foreign to my tastes. Though I took a photo of the iconic Grand Ole Opry in Nashville (Image: Grand Ole Opry), I never actually attended a concert at that legendary venue which many country music enthusiasts would consider worth a pilgrimage.

However, as time went on and I was exposed to more country music, my perspective began to change. I found myself listening to it more frequently and, eventually, started to appreciate it. What had once seemed strange, gradually became something I enjoyed; and I found myself drawn to the timeless sounds of artists like Johnny Cash, Willie Nelson, Dolly Parton, Emmylou Harris, Linda Ronstadt, and Kenny Rogers. Even now, as I reflect on my time in Nashville, I continue to enjoy the rich storytelling and heartfelt melodies of country music, a genre I never expected to grow so fond of.

As for the relationship with the American girl I had come to visit, this unfortunately ended in a disappointment, mostly due to my own inexperience, and that led me to concentrate on my new aspiration: I wanted to study theology at an Adventist university. However, in order to fulfill that ambition, I had to meet two key requirements: improve my English, which was still quite deficient, and pass the General Education Development (GED) test, an indispensable prerequisite for college admission.

To improve my English, I enrolled in an English Composition course at Peabody College in Nashville, now part of Vanderbilt University. I worked diligently to improve my language skills, and my efforts paid off. I also successfully passed the GED test with an impressive percentile rank of 83.6, qualifying me for admission to what is now known as Southern Adventist University (Image: Southern Missionary College), located in the small town of Collegedale near Chattanooga, Tennessee.

It was during my time at this College that I met Theodoros, or Ted as he was commonly known, a Greek student who had come to America for heart surgery and decided to stay for good. Ted was intelligent, good-looking, and highly extroverted, always on the lookout for attractive girls. We became friends, and I learned a lot from Ted, particularly in the realm of social interactions and self-confidence (Image: Ted Mamoulelis).

To help finance our college education, Ted and I worked at night on the assembly line at the nearby McKee Baking Company from 10 p.m. to 2 a.m. Ted, whose family lived in California, was in Tennessee only temporarily, for just one semester. After completing my first semester in Collegedale, I moved to Knoxville for the summer break to earn money for the following semester's tuition. During my time in Knoxville, two memorable incidents stood out.

One weekend, I joined a youth group on a trip to the Smokey Mountains National Park (Image: Smokey Mountains), located east of the Tennessee River. The

Smokey Mountains, part of the Appalachian range, got their name from the natural fog that often hovers over the park. I remember that during the trip, the group leader brought along a large watermelon, which he placed in a river to cool off for a couple of days. After retrieving it, we all enjoyed a refreshing treat together.

During our trip, the group had an unexpected encounter with a black mother bear and her two cubs. As the cubs climbed a tree, the mother bear stood at the bottom, guarding her young. Eager for a better view, I got too close to the tree, causing the mother bear to take a few threatening steps forward. Startled, I quickly retreated, realizing how dangerous the situation could have become.

In Knoxville, I also witnessed a historic moment on television: the Apollo 11 moon landing on July 20, 1969. The whole world watched as Neil Armstrong and Buzz Aldrin made their first steps on the lunar surface, accompanied by Armstrong's famous words, "That's one small step for man, one giant leap for mankind."

While many evangelical Americans at the time believed that such an event was beyond God's permission, seeing it as an intrusion into the heavenly realm, I did not share that skepticism. Instead, I was filled with curiosity, hoping to see if the landing would be successful and whether the astronauts would return safely to Earth.

One day, my friend Ted visited me in Knoxville and convinced me not to return to Chattanooga. Instead, he suggested that I join him in California for further studies. After some consideration, I agreed. Ted called his brother Manuel in California, asking him to bring the family car to Tennessee so the three of us could drive across the United States together.

The three of us first traveled back to Chattanooga to gather my and Ted's belongings before embarking on an extended road trip. Our first stop was Huntsville, Alabama, where we visited the Space Center and learned more about the Apollo missions. We saw a replica of the famous Eagle, the Apollo Lunar Module, which Armstrong and Aldrin had used to land on the moon (Images: At the Huntsville Space Center).

From Huntsville, we continued our journey to Atlanta, Georgia, before heading south to Miami Beach. I vividly remember the sight of the tall Florida royal palms lining the coast, swaying gently in the breeze. In Miami, we spent a few days soaking up the sun on the beautiful white sand beaches

 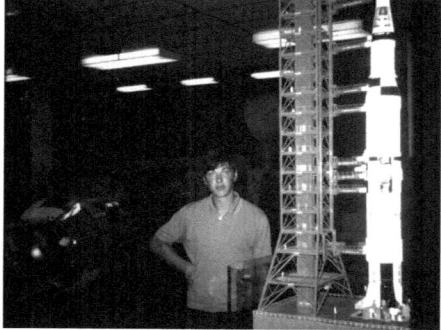

18

and also visited the Everglades National Park (Image: Everglades National Park).

As we made our way across the country, the three of us took turns driving, enabling us to travel both day and night. One of us would drive for four hours while another sat in the passenger seat, and the third would sleep in the back of the old Ford to rest up. We occasionally stopped to buy food along the way and would have breakfast on the trunk of the car, enjoying the simplicity and freedom of our trip (Image: Eating on the car trunk). The long journey across the United States became an unforgettable adventure, one that I would cherish for years to come.

From Miami, we continued our journey north along the Atlantic Ocean, eager to explore more of what the East Coast had to offer. Our first major stop

was at the Kennedy Space Center at Cape Canaveral, where we marveled at the iconic spaceport that had launched the Apollo rockets. Standing in the presence of so much history and space exploration, I couldn't help but feel awe-struck by the achievements of mankind in the race to the stars (Image: Cape Canaveral).

Next, we stopped at Daytona Beach, where we enjoyed another refreshing swim in the Atlantic Ocean. The warm waters and the wide stretch of beach made for a relaxing and fun break from our long drive. After spending the weekend at Daytona, we continued our adventure, heading north to Washington D.C. The capital city, brimming with historical and political significance, offered a wealth of sightseeing opportunities.

In Washington D.C., we visited some of the most famous landmarks of the United States. We stood in front of the majestic Jefferson Memorial, admired the grandeur of the Lincoln Memorial, and marveled at the towering Washington Monument. We also explored the Capitol building (Image: At the Capitol) and visited the White House (Image), imagining the history that had unfolded in these very places.

From Washington, we continued our journey to the Big Apple, New York City. However, we only spent a single day there, as we felt little inclination to stay longer in the bustling and expensive city. After taking in a few sights, we moved on to Buffalo City to visit the Niagara Falls (Image next page: At the Niagara Falls), where the waters of Lake Erie flow into Lake Ontario. The spectacle was an impressive sight to behold and to be remembered. Unfortunately, we couldn't cross the Rainbow Bridge into Canada to view the Horseshoe Falls from the Canadian side, as we did not have the necessary visa, which we couldn't obtain on such short notice.

Undeterred, we continued our journey, traveling through Pennsylvania and Ohio, making our way to Indiana, where we visited Andrews University in Berrien Springs (near Benton Harbor). We spent the weekend here at this Adventist institution, and little did I know then that I would return to Andrews University four years later for my graduate studies.

Our journey then took us to Chicago, and from there, we drove across the Midwest, passing through Illinois, Iowa, Minnesota, and South Dakota, before reaching the Western region of the United States. In Wyoming, Idaho, and Nevada, we explored the vast landscapes, and in the Rocky Mountains, stopped at Yellowstone National Park where we saw the "Old Faithful" Geyser which erupts about every hour (Image: Old Faithful Geyser). Here, we also had some encounters with Grizzly bears, who came so close to our car that it almost seemed as if they might reach inside (Image: Yellowstone Bear).

As we continued westward, we reached Reno, Nevada, and finally entered California. Bypassing Sacramento, we made our way to our ultimate destination: *Pacific Union College*, located near the village of Angwin in the picturesque Napa Valley. The long road trip had taken us all across the United States, with unforgettable experiences and memories along the way.

California

Arriving in California and nearing San Francisco, I was reminded of Scott McKenzie's best-selling single "San Francisco" ("Be sure to Wear Flowers in Your Hair"), appraising the hippie movement which in 1967 had its "Summer of Love" in down town San Francisco. Even as far away as in Berlin I had sensed the liberating spirit and enchanting melodies of that hippie generation.

But the hippie movement was not welcomed by everybody. Only two years later – at the time we arrived in California – that counter culture had come under criticism for all its drug abuse (mostly Marijuana and LSD), anti-Vietnam-war rhetoric and defiance of American patriotism. That year (1969), Merle Haggard, the famous country music singer, in his hit "I am an Okie from Muskogee," set a disapproving counterpoint by singing "We don't smoke marijuana in Muskogee, we don't take our trips on LSD, we don't burn our draft cards down in Mainstreet. … We don't let our hair grow long and shaggy like the hippies out in San Francisco do."

How should I relate to this American counter-culture movement? As a German, I wasn't sure; I was too preoccupied in getting settled and registered at my new College and had no time or desire to learn more about the pros and cons of this anti-establishment culture. It was too foreign to me, at that time. Besides, I never had any inclination to let my hair grow long or take any kind of drugs. But I did once demonstrate against the Vietnam war (while still in Berlin).

My time at Pacific Union College (PUC) was intense, balancing both academic and financial responsibilities. Normally, completing a college degree took four years, but having already spent one semester at Southern College in Chattanooga, Tennessee, I spent just three years at PUC to graduate. I pursued a double major in Theology and German and finished my Bachelor of Arts with *magna cum laude*.

To fund my education, I had to work some 20 hours a week in various campus jobs. I spent time in the college kitchen washing dishes or mixing granola for breakfast. Occasionally, I worked outdoors, raking autumn leaves in the college gardens. During the summer months I worked as a "colporteur," selling books from door to door. Though challenging, that job helped me earn just enough money to start each new school year.

My summer job took me to several Californian cities, including Lodi, Stockton, Modesto, Turlock, Merced, and Fresno. I also had the opportunity to visit San Francisco and Los Angeles multiple times. On weekends, we occasionally escaped to Yosemite National Park, famous for its stunning landscapes, including the iconic Half Dome, which looks like a massive granite dome sliced in half (Image: Half Dome). Yosemite was also home to some of the largest and oldest trees in California. The park's wildlife, particularly the deer, had grown so accustomed to human presence that they would approach people fearlessly, making for an unforgettable experience (Image: Yosemite Deer)

One of my summer breaks turned into an unforgettable adventure when I accepted the invitation from a Swedish fellow student to explore Arizona in a rented camper. We first set off along State Route 1, the legendary highway that hugs California's Pacific coastline all the way down to Los Angeles. As the longest route in California, it offers some of the most scenic ocean views in the world, with dramatic cliffs, rolling waves, and picturesque seaside towns.

About halfway down the coast, we made a stop at the famous Hearst Castle, an architectural marvel perched atop the hills of San Simeon. Built by publishing tycoon William Randolph Hearst and designed by renowned architect Julia Morgan, the opulent estate is a masterpiece of grandeur and excess, something rarely to be encountered in the U.S. The castle features grand halls and lavish suites filled with priceless art and antiques from across the world. It also features the Neptune Pool—an outdoor swimming pool framed by classical colonnades and adorned with statues offering a majestic view of the Pacific Ocean—, and the Roman Pool, an indoor bath lined with deep blue and gold mosaic tiles, evoking the elegance of an ancient Roman spa.

Beautifully landscaped gardens surround the mansion, providing breathtaking panoramic views. Now preserved as a museum and state park, Hearst Castle draws countless visitors fascinated by its rich history, architectural splendor, and the extravagant lifestyle of its original owner. For me, the visit to Hearst Castle was a glimpse into a bygone era of American wealth, power, and artistic ambition—a stark contrast to my own modest student life.

From Hearst Castle, we went east to the Death Valley National Park, one of the hottest places on Earth (Image: Death Valley). There, we visited Badwater Basin, the lowest point in North America at 282 feet (86 m) below sea level. From there, we made our way to Las Vegas, Nevada, where we briefly indulged in the city's famous slot machines and one-armed bandits before heading east to the Hoover Dam, a marvel of 1930s engineering. The dam, built to control the Colorado River, created Lake Mead, the largest reservoir in the U.S. by water capacity, stretching over 100 miles and plunging more than 500 feet deep.

Our next major stop was the Grand Canyon, the natural wonder that displays millions of years of geological history in its vast rock layers. To witness the canyon at its most stunning, we arrived very early in the morning as

the rising sun painted the rock formations in a breathtaking mix of light and shadow (Image: Kurt and Grand Canyon)

Determined to reach the Colorado River, my Swedish friend proposed hiking down, while I preferred to take a mule. We agreed on a simple rule— if two mules were available, we'ld ride; otherwise, we'ld hike. As fate would have it, only one mule was available, so we both set off on foot. We took the Bright Angel Trail, an eight-mile descent into the canyon. Knowing the uphill return hike would be brutal, I rushed downhill in exactly 2 hours and 5 minutes, while my Swedish fellow student followed five minutes behind.

After cooling off with a swim in the Colorado River (Image: Swimming in the Colorado River) and enjoying our packed food, we braced for the grueling ascent. My Swedish friend completed the return hike in five hours, while I, feeling the strain, finished the ordeal in six hours (Image: Ascent). The intense trek left me sore for a full week, but both of us felt an immense sense of accomplishment.

Our journey continued southeast to the famous Arizona Meteor Crater, near Flagstaff (Image). With a diameter of over one kilometer and a depth of 170 meters, this massive impact site was formed about 50,000 years ago when a 50-meter-wide meteorite crashed into Earth at 15-30 km per second. The impact is estimated to have ejected 175 million tons of debris, causing a

5.5-magnitude earthquake, and to have wiped out all life within a four-kilometer radius. The Barringer Crater, as it is also known, is considered one of the best-preserved meteor craters on Earth. Needless to say, we had to climb down to the crater's center, and walked up again to continue our journey.

From there, we ventured north into Southern Utah, where we explored two more breathtaking landscapes: Bryce Canyon National Park, famous for its unique, towering rock spires known as hoodoos;

and Zion National Park, a geologist's paradise with steep red cliffs, deep canyons, and breathtaking trails (Image: Zion Park). Our trip was not just

a road adventure but also an education in geology, endurance, and exploration.

During my time at Pacific Union College, I enjoyed the friendship with a number of fellow students (Image). But I also had the privilege of learning from some exceptional professors.

Among them was Dr. Fred Veltman, who guided me through the intricacies of New Testament Greek, and Dr. Eric Syme, a historian whose eloquence made the past come alive. Carl Coffman instilled in me the art of

homiletics (i.e. preaching), while Dr. Herbert Stoeger, an Austrian professor of both psychology and German, not only broadened my academic horizons but also gave me a personality test the result of which he described as a "rigid personality," which in effect meant I should open up more emotionally.

During my first year at PUC, I was the only German student on campus. However, the following year, I was joined by Rudi Maier, a fellow countryman who would later go on to earn a PhD, serve as a missionary in Sri Lanka, teach at Andrews University in Michigan, and eventually become the international CEO of the Adventist Development and Relief Agency (ADRA). Our shared background and experiences forged a lasting friendship that has endured through the years until today. He now lives near Chattanooga, Tennessee.

At one point, I began dating a strikingly beautiful fellow student. She had a close friend, and in the spirit of camaraderie, my friend Ted—whom I had gotten to know in Tennessee—decided to date that friend, creating a balanced quartet. However, as time passed, I found myself unable or unwilling to fully open up, recognizing that true intimacy required a level of vulnerability I was not yet prepared to display. Aware that the relationship could not thrive under such circumstances, I made the difficult decision to end it.

Ted, on the other hand, took a different path. For the first time, he remained entirely devoted to his partner, ultimately marrying her. Their bond lasted a lifetime, and they stayed together until his passing—proof that sometimes, love finds its way even in the most unexpected of beginnings.

In 1972, I graduated from Pacific Union College with a Bachelor of Arts in Theology and German and graduated with cap and gown, as is common practice in the States. (Image: Ted Mamoulelis, PUC President Floyed Rittenhouse and Kurt). A major step in my academic career had been taken.

Through hard work, determination, and a sense of adventure, I made the most of my college years, setting the stage for the next chapter of my journey.

I also applied for and received a scholarship toward my tuition at Andrews University, where I planned to pursue my graduate studies. But before continuing my education, I wanted to fulfill yet another long-held dream of mine of visiting Africa, a continent that had fascinated me ever since hearing stories from missionaries who had lived there.

27

Pacific Union College had a "student missionary" program that allowed students to spend a year at a mission station, covering their own travel costs while receiving free room and board but no salary. I decided to participate and committed myself to spending a year in Togo, West Africa. When researching flights, I discovered that a return ticket to West Africa was as expensive as a round-the-world ticket. Seizing the opportunity, I purchased a round-the-world ticket from PanAm, the renowned American airline that operated from 1927 until its bankruptcy in 1991. The ticket allowed me to interrupt my journey as often as I wanted, provided I continued traveling eastward. The price was exactly 1500 dollars.

Back to Europe

I booked a flight via Los Angeles to Paris. Before leaving, however, I reached out to a striking blonde I had met before, asking her if she was willing to show me around Los Angeles. She agreed, and together we set off to explore the city. Our first stop was the "Queen Mary," the majestic ocean liner that once ruled the North Atlantic from 1936 to 1967. Now permanently docked at Long Beach, it had been transformed into a museum, hotel, and restaurant. At over 300 meters long and towering more than 180 meters high, the "Queen Mary" dwarfed even the legendary "Titanic". Walking its grand decks, I could almost hear echoes of a bygone era, when the world's elite crossed the Atlantic in unparalleled luxury (Image: Queen Mary).

Next, we visited Disneyland, an experience that defied easy description. (Image: Disney Land) The park overflowed with wonders, from its thrilling rides to its immersive worlds. Of all the attractions, two left the deepest impression on me—"Pirates of the Caribbean," with its lifelike animatronic buccaneers and hauntingly atmospheric scenes, and "The Haunted Mansion," where eerie illusions and ghostly apparitions blurred the line between fantasy and reality. We also made time for a visit to Loma Linda Hospital, a renowned Adventist medical center, before attending a church service at the Loma Linda Church.

I then kissed good bye to the blond, and boarded the plane to Paris. Having arrived in Paris, I wanted to visit my parents in the Palatinate region. But rather than purchasing a train ticket to Germany, I decided to hitchhike in an effort to save money. I managed to get a ride to Lille in northern France, where I was unable to find another lift. Undeterred, I made my way on foot to the train station, carrying my heavy suitcase, and bought a ticket to Aachen, where I knew my brother Bernd was living. Upon arriving, however, I discovered that Bernd had relocated to Düsseldorf just days earlier. I phoned him, and he gladly came to pick me up.

As luck would have it, our parents were planning to come to Düsseldorf the very next day, completely unaware of the surprise awaiting them. When they arrived, Bernd greeted them with a knowing smile and said, "I have a surprise for you." My mother, almost instinctively, exclaimed, "Kurt is here!?" And there I was, reunited with my family after four long years of absence. The reunion was filled with stories of my experiences in the U.S., but I also had news of my next adventure—as I planned to spend a year in Africa.

Before heading to Togo, however, I hoped to fulfill yet another dream: attending the 1972 Olympic Games in Munich as a visitor. The Munich Games were special. What was meant to be a celebration of international sportsmanship and unity had turned into one of the darkest moments in Olympic history. During the Games, eight Palestinian terrorists infiltrated the Olympic Village, killing two members of the Israeli Olympic team and taking nine others hostage. A failed German police rescue attempt resulted in the deaths of all the hostages, along with five of the eight terrorists. The tragedy sent shockwaves around the world, and the Games were paused for an entire day in mourning.

It was that one day pause which gave me the opportunity to witness the final event of the Games on its very last day. Borrowing my father's car, I drove to Munich and attended the team event of equestrian show jumping at the big Olympic Stadium. In a thrilling competition, Germany secured the gold medal, edging out the United States by a mere 0.25 points. One of the leading German equestrians was Hans Günter Winkler, perhaps the best equestrian of all times, who won his 5th Olympic gold medal in Munich.

The Munich Games were also marked by the phenomenal achievements of American swimmer Mark Spitz, who won a total of seven gold medals— each with a new world record—cementing his status as the star of the Games. Another standout was Soviet gymnast Olga Korbut, whose grace and daring routines captivated audiences as she claimed three gold medals.

An unforgettable moment at the Munich games, certainly from a German perspective, was the stunning gold medal victory of high jumper Ulrike Meyfarth. Just 16 years old, she was a relative unknown, yet she made history by becoming the youngest-ever Olympic champion in her event and one of the first Europeans to adopt the revolutionary Fosbury Flop technique—rather than the traditional straddle. With 1.92 meters, Meyfarth not only secured the gold medal with remarkable composure and style, but also set a new world record and a new Olympic record. Her triumph was a defining moment of the Games, inspiring a new generation of high jumpers. Remarkably, Meyfarth would repeat her feat 12 years later at the 1984 Olympic Games in Los Angeles, where she claimed another gold medal at the age of 28, this time clearing an impressive 2.02 meters. Her career remains one of the most extraordinary in Olympic history.

Despite the tragedy that had overshadowed the Munich event, these moments of athletic brilliance remained a testament to the resilience and spirit of the Olympic Games. I was happy to have caught a glimpse of that spirit by attending the very last event and also the closing ceremony.

Discovering Africa

Following my brief visit to Germany, I took a train to Paris, where I boarded a flight to Lomé, Togo, to begin my year as a student missionary. However, upon arrival, I learned that the missionary I was supposed to stay with had recently moved to what was then called Upper Volta (now Burkina Faso).

Burkina Faso was a landlocked nation in the sub-Saharan savanna of West Africa. Its landscape, dominated by grasslands, woodlands, and semi-arid bushlands (Image next page: Upper Volta), was shaped by cycles of fire and grazing. Even today, Burkina Faso remains one of the world's least developed countries. It shares borders with Mali, Niger, Benin, Togo, and Ghana. Its territory is larger than West Germany at the time of my visit.

I continued my journey to Ouagadougou, the capital city, where I stayed with Henri Kempf and his family. Originally from Alsace-Lorraine, the Kempfs were in the process of establishing an evangelistic center while also seeking to provide agricultural training to support local development. I was asked to assist Henri in any way possible to help set up the new Adventist center (Image: Henri and Kurt and two local co-workers).

The Mossi people formed the most prominent ethnic group of this country (Image: Mossi man) – alongside the Fulanis and the Tuaregs. The Fulani women were striking in their elegant attire (Image: Fulani woman), while the Tuareg men, known as the "blue men of the desert," covered their faces almost entirely, revealing only their eyes (Image: Tuareg man).

At one point, we formed a bond with a Tuareg family, and I had the joy of holding their beautiful baby boy in my arms (Image: Kurt and Tuareg baby). Later, with quite sorrow, I learned that the child had passed away – a heartbreaking testament to the high infant mortality in West Africa. When I admired the father's finely crafted sword, he did not pause for even a breath before placing it in my hands as a gift. I was stunned, touched beyond words. These people did not hold tightly to possessions. He knew he could forge another. But a week later, he approached me with a humble request: might I help him obtain a fine cloth from the market? It was a request I could not refuse. He chose a beautiful, high-quality fabric—its value clear in price and craftmanship (Image: Kurt and Tuareg man). At one point, the friendly Tuareg man even dressed me up like a Tuareg (Image: Tuareg man and Kurt)

Islam was the predominant religion in Upper Volta, with Christianity present in some communities, while many natives, particularly in the rural southwest, practiced traditional animistic beliefs. During major Islamic celebrations, vast gatherings of Mossi people convened for prayers (Image: Muslims praying), and the Festival of Sacrifice was marked by the ritual slaughter of goats and sheep.

The country's former name, "Upper Volta," stemmed from the three major rivers that traverse its land: the Black Volta, the White Volta, and the Red Volta (Image:Volta River). Food insecurity was widespread, and at every turn I was confronted with the stark reality of malnourished children with their typical protuberant bellies due to inadequate protein intake (Kwarshiorkor) (Image: malnourished children). Though the region was home to diverse wildlife, my only encounter with animals was limited to crocodiles (Image: Kurt and Crocodile).

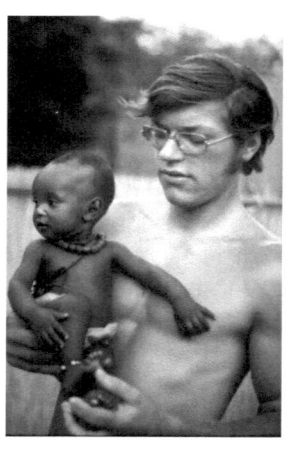

The Mossi culture was deeply oral, with village elders passing down ancestral knowledge through spoken word rather than written records. Music and dance played a vital role in daily life, with traditional drums serving both as instruments of rhythm and long-distance communication. In the evenings, I witnessed village men dancing around open fires, their movements so fervent that they seemed to lose awareness of their surroundings, as if in trance. (Image previous page: dancers)

During my stay in Ouagadougou, French President Georges Pompidou paid an official state visit to Upper Volta (Image previous page: Pompidou), an event that transformed the city into a vibrant spectacle of culture and tradition. Countless groups from across the country flocked to the capital, dressed in elaborate, age-old ethnic attire, performing traditional dances and music to honor the occasion. I had never before witnessed such a breathtaking display of cultural diversity—what had once seemed a subdued and austere country suddenly burst into a dazzling mosaic of colors, rhythms, and traditions (Images: traditional groups). That evening, during the state banquet at the Presidential Palace, the Kempf family and I were among the invited guests, an experience that added yet another remarkable memory to my time in West Africa.

Despite these vivid impressions, I found myself feeling somewhat out of place in Upper Volta. The Kempf family, fluent in French, English, and German, spoke mostly in German to me, limiting my opportunities to practice French. Moreover, I often struggled to find a true sense of purpose in my daily activities. Seeking new experiences, I took the opportunity to travel to Ghana, where I spent several weeks.

The northern part of Ghana bore a striking resemblance to Upper Volta's semi-arid savanna, but as I ventured further southward, the landscape transformed dramatically. Dense rainforests and lush green vegetation replaced the dry terrain, offering an entirely different environment (Image). English, widely spoken as Ghana's *lingua franca*, made communication far easier, allowing me to engage more freely with the people and immerse myself more deeply in the local culture.

During my time in Ghana, I first traveled to Bolgatanga in the northern region before continuing by bus to Tamale. Although the bus was already filled to capacity, the conductor still allowed me to board, and the passengers graciously shifted to make room. I found myself seated next to a charming Ghanaian woman—an encounter that remains vivid in my memory (Image: Woman).

In Tamale, I became involved in an evangelistic campaign, which gave me a chance to engage with the local Christian community and experience the vibrant spirituality of the region. (Image: Kurt and Ghanaean students) On one occasion, I was invited to preach to a congregation, a majority of whom spoke little to no English.

This meant that my words had to be translated first into one local language, then into a second. As a result, my talk took three times longer than it would have without the need for translation. The process was slow but unavoidable.

From Tamale, I journeyed further southward to Kumasi, the historical and cultural heartland of the Ashanti people. The route to Kumasi included a memorable crossing of the expansive Volta Lake by boat—an experience that added a scenic and reflective pause to the journey. (Image next page:

Ferry) Not far from Kumasi, I made a heartfelt stop in Atibie, where I paid a visit to an Adventist hospital. Nestled amid lush greenery, the Kwahu Hospital provided not only medical care to the people of the region, but also a familiar face. The physician in charge, Dr. Sherman Nagel, had been my biology professor at Pacific Union College before answering a call in 1972 to serve as a medical missionary in Ghana (Image: Dr. Nagel).

 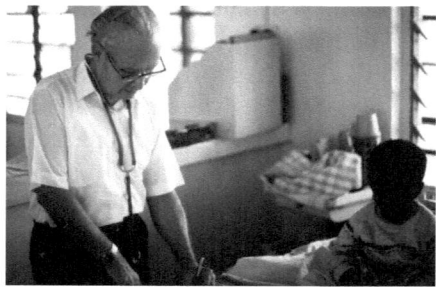

Dr. Nagel allowed me to observe several surgical procedures in the operating theatre—a rare and fascinating experience. Among the cases I witnessed was a Caesarean section, an awe-inspiring moment as I saw a newborn emerge directly from the mother's womb. Another case involved a post-Caesarean patient suffering from internal bleeding, requiring Dr. Nagel to reopen the surgical wound in an intense and meticulous procedure. Watching these operations gave me a deep respect for the skills of this doctor committed to keep people healthy and save their lives.

During my time at the Kwahu Hospital, I also became acquainted with an American cultural anthropologist who was conducting his field research on the Ashanti people. This ethnologist, intent on writing his PhD on the rich traditions of the Ashantis, had immersed himself deeply in their culture. Living among them, he spoke their language fluently and sought to understand their way of life, beliefs, and customs. He shared with me his firm conviction that the only true way to grasp the essence of an ethnic group was to live amongst them, speak their language, and become an integral part of their community.

With the anthropologist's guidance, I had the opportunity to attend the funeral of a prominent local leader—an event that would provide me with a vivid and colorful glimpse into Ashanti life. The funeral, over which the Chief presided, was a grand and vibrant affair, with mourners adorned in their finest Kente cloth dresses (Images: Funeral with tribal Chief). For the Ashanti people, such funerals are the most significant and ceremonial occasions in their culture, and the procession was a memorable spectacle of color and tradition.

On another occasion, also arranged by the anthropologist, I was honored with an invitation to observe a council of elders—once again under the dignified leadership of the community's Chief. The gathering revealed a striking form of governance and communication, steeped in tradition and symbolism. Rather than addressing the assembly directly, the Chief spoke in a hushed tone to his spokesman, who then projected the message with clarity and authority to those gathered.

The ritual reminded me of biblical scenes—where divine words are conveyed through a chosen mediator to the people. It echoed the ancient, and at times still-practiced, ways in which tribal leaders communicate with their communities: not with volume, but through the sanctity of structure.

Through moments like these, I came to witness the profound richness of the Ashanti culture—its layers of meaning, its intricate social fabric, and the time-honored customs that continue to shape communal life.

The anthropologist was just one of several visitors whom I encountered in Atibie/Kwahu. On one occasion, another American arrived with his wife to support the work of the hospital. I don't recall what he had been assigned to do, but I remember the tragic event that followed soon after their arrival. Just days into their stay, the wife set off on a short trip, and tragically, the car she was traveling in was involved in a head-on collision when an oncoming vehicle, overtaking around a blind bend, struck them. She died instantly, leaving her husband in a state of shock and bewilderment at the sudden and senseless loss.

From the Ashanti region, I returned to Ouagadougou to further assist Henry Kempf in his effort to establish his new center there. But after seven and a half months in Ouagadougou, I decided it was time to bid farewell to the Kempf family and to Ouagadougou and begin my journey back to California.

My first stop was Abidjan, the capital of the Ivory Coast at the time, where I spent only a couple of days exploring the bustling city. Wandering through its vibrant marketplace, I marveled at the abundance of tropical fruits, especially the delicious mangos. During my time in Ouagadougou, I had developed a deep appreciation for the rich, sweet flavor of mangos, but in Abidjan, I discovered a specimen so magnificent that it seemed almost mythical, and I purchased and consumed this most succulent mango I had ever eaten. Reflecting on the biblical account of Adam and Eve, I liked to jest that the forbidden fruit could not have been an apple—nowhere mentioned in Genesis—but must have been a mango, its irresistible taste so alluring that it led to mankind's fateful first transgression. Succumbing to its temptation myself, I devoured the fruit with great delight, only to fall ill a few days later—perhaps a consequence of my indulgence, adding a humorous twist to my own version of the paradise story.

Before leaving Abidjan, I was determined to capture a perfect nighttime photograph of the Pont Félix Houphouët-Boigny, the striking bridge spanning the lagoon. To achieve the best vantage point, I sought access to one of the city's towering skyscrapers. Boldly, I rang the bell of the topmost apartment and explained my request to the resident. To my surprise, the occupant, a distinguished French gentleman, not only welcomed me in but graciously gave me a tour of his luxurious two-storey penthouse. From the top floor, I was able to take the photographs I had envisioned, admiring the breathtaking view of the illuminated cityscape (Image: Pont Félix Houphouët-Boigny).

Expressing my gratitude with a heartfelt "Merci beaucoup," I took one last look at Abidjan's dazzling skyline before heading off into the night, unaware that my adventure—and my encounter with the mango—was about to take an unexpected turn.

From the Ivory Coast, it was just a short flight to Accra, the bustling capital of Ghana. However, upon my arrival, I began feeling unwell. A growing fever prompted me to visit a doctor, who quickly diagnosed me with hepatitis A—likely contracted from consuming contaminated food. Immediately, my mind flashed back to the enormous mango I had devoured in Abidjan, suspecting that the delicious fruit may have harbored the virus.

38

Following the doctor's recommendation, I set off for the Kwahu Hospital in Atibie, east of Kumasi, a place I knew would offer a peaceful environment for recuperation.

Upon arrival at the Kwahu Hospital, I entrusted myself into the care of the doctors and hoped for a swift recovery. I was placed in the Kwahu Hospital's small guest house, isolated to ensure I wouldn't spread the highly contagious virus. It was a lonely time, but I appreciated the solitude as it allowed me to rest and recover. Another American doctor and his family,

who were at the hospital as well, took it upon themselves to cook meals for me, offering me comfort during my quarantine. Their kindness was a beacon in a time when I could not interact with others. After three weeks of recovery, I regained my strength and was healthy enough to resume my journey, grateful for the care and the acts of kindness that had supported me through my illness.

My journey took me from Accra to Lomé in Togo where I enjoyed the wonderful beach (Image: Kurt in Togo), and then on to Cotonou, the capital of Benin, which was still known as Dahomey at the time. I spent a few days exploring the city, where I met a charming African lady who kindly invited me to stay with her family.

From there, I ventured to the famous lake village of Ganvié, situated on Lake Nokoué, a lagoon fed by both the Ocean and the Ouéme River. Known as the largest lake village in the region, Ganvié is a unique place where most of the wooden houses are built on stilts (Image: Ganvié, Benin). The

village was established in the 16th or 17th century by people seeking refuge from European enslavers. Often called the "Venice of Africa," the village's aquatic lifestyle is its most notable feature, though the two cities share little else in common. Despite the remote and primitive nature of life in Ganvié, I was both surprised and amused to find that even in such an isolated setting, I could purchase a Coca Cola—an ironic symbol of global modernity amid the village's traditional ways.

After spending a few days in Cotonou, I flew to Lagos, Nigeria, just 120 kilometers away. I had been advised to visit Ibadan, a large city to the north of Lagos, which was said to be more interesting than the capital itself. I spent some time exploring the local market, a fascinating place brimming with cultural treasures (Image: Ibaden Market, Nigeria). Here, I  discovered a variety of jujus—amulets and charms used across West Africa for healing physical or psychological ailments, or to cast or protect against spells.

It was in Nigeria that I also learned an important lesson in overcoming my own biases. Upon arriving at Lagos airport, I had been required to exchange a certain amount of money into the local currency (Naira), with the understanding that any unused funds could be converted back into US dollars before leaving. When it came time for me to board my flight to Nairobi, I found that I had some Naira left, worth about 20 US-Dollars—for me, at the time, not a negligible sum. However, I was told they didn't have the cash to exchange the Naira back into dollars, but could transfer the amount via bank transfer. I hesitated. Having encountered many attempts to cheat me during my travels, I doubted whether I would ever see the money again. Reluctantly, I gave them the remaining Naira as well as my bank account number, expecting only the worst. But months later, back in the States, when checking my bank statement, I was pleasantly surprised to find the 20 dollars had indeed been transferred from Nigeria into my account. While grateful for the money, the experience also left me with a valuable lesson: Never let your own biases and prejudices cloud your judgment.

From Lagos I flew to Nairobi, where I spent time exploring the city (Images: Nairobi by day and by night), and I also took an excursion to the Nairobi National Park, located just outside the Kenyan capital. The park was home to a variety of wildlife, and I saw zebras, giraffes, antelopes, monkeys, wild boars and even a cheetah, which delighted me very much.

While in Kenya, there was a total solar eclipse, which I could have witnessed had I traveled about 200 kilometers north. However, I felt the trip wasn't worth my time or money. So instead, I stayed in Nairobi and witnessed only a partial solar eclipse on June 30, 1973, where 93 percent of the sun was obscured by the moon. Unfortunately, a partial eclipse is far less impressive than the spectacle of a total eclipse. I would have to wait for another such opportunity.

From Nairobi I flew on to Addis Abeba, the capital of Ethiopia, where the people looked strikingly different from those in sub-Saharan Africa. Their facial features stood apart, and the atmosphere was far less welcoming than what I had experienced in West Africa or Kenya. What particularly struck me was the way Ethiopian women carried their loads: While women across much of Africa typically balanced heavy bundles on their heads with upright posture (Image: Ghanaean woman), Ethiopian women carried their burdens on their backs, bent over in a stoop. To me, that was a rather somber sight (Image: Ethiopian woman).

Furthermore, in other countries, when I attempted to photograph peo-

ple, they usually smiled, waved, or even crowded in front of me, eager for their pictures to be taken. However, in Ethiopia, most people resented being photographed, their annoyance clearly visible.

41

In Addis, I passed by the palace of Ethiopian Emperor Haile Selassie, who would remain in power for just one more year before being overthrown in a military coup in 1974, backed by the Soviet Union. But even during my visit, I could feel an undercurrent of unrest, a sense of revolt brewing in the air. The emperor was eventually imprisoned by the military junta and assassinated in 1975. His remains were recovered in 2000 and reburied at the Holy Trinity Cathedral in Addis Abeba—a cathedral I visited during my stay, noting also the opulent chair reserved for the Emperor (Image: Throne).

I also attended a Sunday church service at the Holy Trinity Cathedral which belongs to the Ethiopian Orthodox Church. During the church service, the priest took the large Bible from the altar and walked through the rows of worshippers so they could kiss it. When he noticed me standing at the back, he gave me a stern and disapproving look. I realized that I had inadvertently stood on the side reserved for women, so I moved to the other side of the church, where only men were permitted to worship.

I also ventured south of Addis Abeba, where the landscape shifted dramatically, displaying a completely different environment (Images: Ethiopian landscapes). During my travels, I also had the chance to taste traditional Ethiopian food, particularly injira—the sour, fermented pancake-like flatbread with a spongy texture, made from teff flour. Teff, a cereal grass that grows mainly in Ethiopia and Eritrea, is a staple of the local diet. Injira is often served with a delicious stew containing vegetables and meat such as chicken, beef, or lamb. I found myself thoroughly enjoying this unique dish, which is traditionally eaten with one's hands, adding to the rich cultural experience.

Around the World

From Addis Ababa, I flew onward to Bombay, now known as Mumbai. As the bus carried me from the airport into the city, I was met with a sight that left me deeply shaken. I had encountered poverty in Africa, but nothing had prepared me for what I would witness here.

In Africa, poverty was largely confined to rural villages, where life was simple, but people at least had a hut to call their own. The land was vast, and even the poorest had space to breathe. But in Bombay, poverty was relentless and all-consuming. Thousands—no, millions—lived on the streets with no shelter, no privacy, no true place to rest. I saw entire families sprawled along sidewalks, their few belongings piled beside them, their sleeping spaces claimed by sheer necessity. When the rains came, as they often did in this part of the world, makeshift plastic sheets became their only defense against the downpour (Image).

Beyond the sidewalks, slum settlements stretched for miles—rows of shacks cobbled together from wooden boards, scrap metal, and whatever materials people could scavenge (Images: slums). And yet, within the same city, opulence flourished. There were grand mansions, lux-

urious villas, and towering apartment buildings, home to the wealthy elite. The contrast between unimaginable wealth and utter destitution was staggering, more extreme than anything I had ever seen. And there were countless beggars hoping for, and often demanding, some small coins of charity.

From Bombay, I took a train to Poona to visit Spicer Memorial College, now known as Spicer Adventist University. It was here that I unexpectedly crossed paths with an American evangelist whose sermon I had heard months earlier at the Loma Linda Church in Los Angeles. When I mentioned this to him, he immediately asked, "Did you like it?"

Caught off guard, I hesitated as I could not truthfully say yes, yet I was too polite to say no. The sermon had lacked the self-critical spirit that for me was indispensable in my search for truth.

"Maybe you didn't like it," he remarked bluntly. I fumbled for a response, offering something vague and noncommittal.

That was the end of our conversation and the beginning of a mutual indifference. He was committed to the traditional Adventist narrative and theology, with all its peculiarities and oddities, while I was yet on the search for truth, unrelenting, uncompromising, unwavering.

After a brief stay in Poona, where I spent the night at Spicer College and explored its surroundings, I boarded a train back to Bombay. From there, I caught a flight to New Delhi, India's sprawling and historic capital (Image: Kurt in Delhi). I took in the city's grand monuments and bustling streets, indulging in the usual sightseeing before continuing my journey to nearby Agra—home to one of the world's most breathtaking architectural masterpieces: the Taj Mahal.

No amount of prior knowledge or photographs could have truly prepared me for its sheer beauty. Commissioned by the Mughal emperor Shah Jahan as a mausoleum for his beloved wife, Mumtaz Mahal, the Taj Mahal is a vision of ethereal elegance. Made entirely of white marble and completed in 1643, it stands as a timeless tribute to love and loss. Considered the pinnacle of Islamic art in India, it attracts over five million visitors each year, all drawn to its graceful domes, intricate inlays, and perfectly symmetrical gardens (Image: Taj Mahal).

I decided to stay overnight in Agra, finding an unassuming but adequate guesthouse for the astonishingly low price of just two US dollars—if my memory serves me right. To explore the city, I hired a rickshaw driver for an entire day, agreeing to what felt like a negligible sum: one US dollar. By evening, grateful for the rider's effort, and feeling that even a dollar was far too little, I handed him double the agreed amount. His expression of gratitude was genuine, and yet, even then, I knew that for me, it was still an almost absurd bargain.

My next flight took me to the small town of Khajuraho in the heart of Madhya Pradesh, a place renowned for its extraordinary temple ruins—many of which have stood for over a thousand years. For centuries, these architectural marvels lay hidden beneath the dense embrace of the Indian jungle, only to be rediscovered in 1838. Dedicated to the deities Shiva, Vishnu, and Ganesha, the temples of Khajuraho stand as a testament to India's rich artistic and spiritual heritage (Image: Khajuraho).

Beyond their religious significance, these temples are famed for their intricate sculptures, which symbolically depict the four fundamental goals of life in Hindu philosophy: *dharma* (righteousness), *kama* (desire and love), *artha* (prosperity), and *moksha* (spiritual liberation). Among the many carvings adorning the temple walls, some stand out for their strikingly sensual and erotic imagery—an aspect that has fascinated, intrigued, and, at times, perplexed visitors from around the world (Image). British author James McConnachie has captured the essence of these sculptures with evocative detail:

"Twisting, broad-hipped and high-breasted nymphs display their generously contoured and bejeweled bodies on exquisitely worked exterior wall panels ... Beside the heavenly nymphs are serried ranks of griffins, guardian deities, and, most notoriously, extravagantly interlocked maithunas—lovemaking couples."

The temple inscriptions suggest that most of these surviving structures were built between 970 and 1030 AD, with additional temples completed in the following decades. Today, the temples of Khajuraho remain not just an architectural wonder but also a profound artistic expression of life's dualities—sacred and sensual, spiritual and earthly—captured in stone for eternity.

Upon arriving in Khajuraho, I found myself in the company of two young and charming Spanish women who were also exploring India. We quickly bonded over our shared sense of adventure and, in an effort to save money, decided to split the cost of a spacious hotel room with four beds. Beyond the famous temples, there was little to detain us in Khajuraho, and by the next day, we were eager to move on. Together, we boarded a flight to Benares—more widely known to Indians as Varanasi.

Nestled along the banks of the sacred Ganges River, Varanasi is one of the world's oldest continuously inhabited cities, with a history stretching back some 2,500 years. It is a city of profound religious significance, particularly for Hindus, who believe that bathing in the holy Ganges cleanses them of past sins and grants spiritual purification. This ritual immersion is more than a mere cleansing of the body—it is a symbolic rebirth, a step toward salvation (Image: bathing men). While one can observe believers bathing in

the river daily, the practice reaches its peak during the *Kumbh Mela*, a grand festival that takes place four times over a 12-year cycle, drawing millions of devotees seeking divine blessings.

For Hindus, dying in Varanasi—or at least having one's remains cremated there—is considered the ultimate passage to *moksha*, liberation from the eternal cycle of birth, death, and rebirth. It is the highest aspiration of every devout Hindu, as well as for many Buddhists. Along the riverbanks, funeral pyres burn continuously, sending the ashes of the departed into the sacred waters, where their souls are believed to be freed from the cycle of samsara.

The city is home to countless temples, each bearing the architectural imprints of different eras. Among them, the Kashi Vishwanath Temple stands out as one of India's holiest shrines. With its resplendent golden spire, this temple is dedicated to Lord Shiva, the god of destruction and transformation. It is said that a visit to Kashi Vishwanath brings one closer to the divine, making it a pilgrimage site of unparalleled spiritual significance.

Varanasi is a city where life and death coexist in a mesmerizing, almost poetic harmony. The flickering flames of the funeral ghats, the haunting chants of priests, the rhythmic splashes of devotees immersing themselves in the river—all of it creates an atmosphere that is at once overwhelming, humbling, and deeply moving.

Varanasi holds profound significance not only for Hindus but also for Buddhists. Just a few kilometers away lies *Sarnath*, where the Buddha is said to have delivered his first sermon after attaining enlightenment under the Bodhi tree in Bodh Gaya. To commemorate this pivotal moment in history, the *Dhamek Stupa* (Image) was erected—a massive, solid cylindrical structure of brick and stone, towering over 40 meters high with a diameter of 28 meters. This sacred site continues to draw pilgrims and scholars alike, seeking a deeper understanding of the Buddha's teachings.

From Varanasi, we flew to Kathmandu, the capital of Nepal—a city unlike any other, with an atmosphere so distinct and enchanting that it felt almost otherworldly. Often referred to as the "Land of the Gods," Kathmandu is a mesmerizing blend of Hindu and Buddhist heritage, where ancient temples and shrines dominate the landscape. The *Durbar Square*, with its bustling market and exquisite temples, stands as the city's historic and cultural heart, showcasing Nepal's most spectacular traditional architecture (Images: Durbar Square, Kathmandu).

No visit to Kathmandu would be complete without exploring its sacred landmarks. The *Pashupatinath Temple*, one of the most revered Hindu temples dedicated to Lord Shiva, exudes an air of deep spiritual reverence, while the *Changunarayan Temple*, with its intricate carvings, is among Nepal's oldest and most significant places of worship. Equally awe-inspiring are the great Buddhist stupas—*Swayambhunath* (often called the *Monkey Temple,* see Image) and *Boudhanath*, both of which are important centers of Tibetan Buddhism.

Here in Nepal, I met some exotic people, a few of whom wore the traditional prayer chain made of 108 rudraksha beads which are associated with

48

the Hindu deity Shiva and are commonly worn for protection (Image: man mit rudraksha chain). The 108 beads appear to have cosmic significance, sometimes referring to the 12 zodiac signs and 9 planets (9 x 12 = 108). I purchased a chain myself and still treasure it even today. I also found a pious man who had committed himself to stay silent for three years and had finished already one (Image: silent monk writing).

During my stay, I had the privilege of meeting an American family who had adopted ten orphans and graciously offered me a place to stay. Their kind-

ness and generosity were a testament to the spirit of compassion that seemed to pervade Kathmandu. At that time, the city was a magnet for Western travelers seeking to escape the hustle and bustle of their home countries, immersing themselves in Eastern philosophy, spirituality, and the pursuit of inner peace. Whether they truly found what they were looking for, I could not say.

For me, and for the two young Spanish women I had been traveling with, Kathmandu marked the end of our shared journey. From here, we each had our own separate destinations to pursue. We exchanged farewells, knowing we would likely never meet again. And we never did.

From Kathmandu, I flew to Calcutta—the teeming, chaotic heart of West Bengal, now known as Kolkata. Had I not already witnessed unimaginable poverty in Bombay and elsewhere, this city might have come as a profound shock. But by now, I had grown accustomed to scenes of extreme deprivation. Still, the destitution of Calcutta had its own harrowing intensity—raw, relentless, and impossible to ignore.

Calcutta was a city of contradictions, a place of desperation and struggle, yet also one of resilience and vitality. It was a city of extreme poverty, yet rich in history, culture, and intellectual heritage. The streets were chaotic and congested, the air thick with pollution, and the buildings worn by time and neglect. Yet, for all its hardships, the city possessed an undeniable pulse—a spirit that refused to be crushed (Image: street scene).

Everywhere, the streets were alive with movement—vendors calling out their wares, rickshaws weaving through traffic (Image: man with umbrella), the smell of street food mingling with the less pleasant odors of urban decay.

The markets were an explosion of colors, textures, and scents, overflowing with fruits, vegetables, and spices. Despite the overwhelming poverty, the people were gracious and warm, their smiles a quiet defiance against the hardships they faced.

While in Calcutta, I found myself drawn into a local cinema—curious to glimpse the spirit of India through its own silver screen. I didn't understand a single word of the dialogue, yet the film spoke a language all its own. It was a tapestry of conflict and longing, of tender love and aching hope. But more than anything, it was a celebration of beauty—radiant faces, sweeping landscapes, and colors so vivid they seemed to defy the muted greys of Calcutta's weary streets. It was as if the film whispered to its audience: life, despite everything, is magnificent and adorned with hidden grace.

No Bollywood movie, I learned, is complete without music. At least six songs wove themselves into the narrative, lifting the story into the realm of the sublime. For a little while, the audience was carried beyond the weight of daily burdens, offered a fantastical escape into a world where joy dances freely and every sorrow finds its melody.

But there was little time for me to truly immerse myself in the city's rhythms. My visit was fleeting, and I barely scratched the surface of Calcutta's vast and layered identity. Yet, one figure loomed large in my mind as I wandered its streets—Mother Teresa. This was the city where she had dedicated her life to the poorest of the poor, tending to those suffering from hunger, disease, and despair. Her work had become almost synonymous with Calcutta itself, embodying both its deepest sorrows and its greatest acts of compassion.

I left the city with a profound sense of awe and unease—humbled by its struggles, inspired by its spirit, and carrying with me the indelible imprint of its contrasts.

From Calcutta, I flew to Rangoon—or Yangon, as it is now officially called. I arrived in the evening, with only a single night in the city before my onward flight the next morning. Time was short, but there was one place I had to see before leaving the city: the *Shwedagon Pagoda*, the luminous heart of Burma's spiritual life (Image: Shwedagon Pagoda).

By night, the Shwedagon Pagoda is a vision of gold and light, its towering, gilded stupa rising 112 meters above the city skyline, glowing beneath the dark sky like an ethereal beacon. Considered the most sacred Buddhist site in Burma, it is said—though unverified—to have been constructed more than 2,600 years ago, making it possibly the oldest Buddhist stupa in the world.

The entrance to the pagoda is flanked by two immense, stylized lion figures, their watchful gaze guarding the sacred space beyond. Within, innumerable smaller golden stupas and intricate shrines pay homage to various Buddhas, their delicate craftsmanship reflecting the devotion and reverence of countless generations (Images: Inside Shwedagon). Pilgrims and monks moved in silent procession, circumambulating the pagoda, murmuring holy texts as they walked. The air was thick with incense, and the soft glow of oil lamps flickered against the gleaming gold surfaces, creating an atmosphere that was at once majestic and serene.

Standing before this awe-inspiring structure, I felt a profound sense of reverence. It was not merely an architectural wonder but a place alive with faith, imbued with centuries of prayer, devotion, and history. The Shwedagon Pagoda is not simply to be seen—it is to be experienced. And in the hushed, golden glow of the Burmese night, I felt its sacred splendor in a way that words could never fully capture.

Early the next morning, I boarded a flight to Bangkok, the vibrant capital of Thailand, where I would spend several days exploring the city's rich cultural and architectural heritage. Bangkok was a place of golden spires, intricate temples, and bustling streets, and its sights are nothing short of mesmerizing (Image: Floating Market).

My itinerary included some of the city's most iconic landmarks. First, there was the Grand Palace, the former royal residence, an opulent complex of gilded halls, intricate carvings, and dazzling stupas, exuding the grandeur of Thai royalty (Image: Grand Palace). Not far from there, I marveled at *Wat Arun*, the Temple of Dawn, its towering 80-meter spire rising above the banks of the Chao Phraya River, adorned with delicate porcelain mosaics that shimmered in the sunlight (Image: Temple of Dawn).

A visit to *Wat Pho* was equally unforgettable. This temple housed Thailand's largest reclining Buddha, a magnificent 46-meter-long gilded statue, its serene expression embodying divine tranquility (Image: Reclining Buddha). Surrounding it were countless smaller Buddha figures, each representing a different facet of Buddhist devotion.

Another highlight was *Wat Traimit*, home to the Golden Buddha, a breathtaking statue weighing 5.5 tons of solid gold. For centuries, its true nature had remained a secret, hidden beneath layers of stucco and colored glass—a disguise meant to protect it from plundering invaders. Only in 1955 was its golden splendor rediscovered, revealing one of Thailand's most treasured relics (Image next page: Golden Buddha).

These, along with countless other temples, markets, and cultural experiences, made my time in Bangkok both enlightening and unforgettable. Little did I know then that this would not be my last visit to the city. In the years to come, Bangkok would become a place I would return to again and again, both alone and with my family.

From Bangkok, I flew to Saigon, the bustling heart of South Vietnam (Image next page: Street Scene), where I spent only a day or so. At the time, the metropolis—now called Ho Chi Minh City—was still teeming with American soldiers, a reminder that a long and grueling war had ravaged the country and was only now nearing its conclusion.

By January 1973, the Paris Peace Accords had been signed, effectively ending America's direct involvement in the war. But the peace was fragile. Once the Americans withdrew, North Vietnam swiftly launched its final offensive, meeting little resistance from the South Vietnamese army. In April 1975 (i.e. 50 years ago at the time of writing this), the war officially ended, and the country was reunified under the rule of the communist North. At the time of my visit, many American soldiers were eager to return home.

Yet, amid the military presence, my eyes were drawn less to the U.S. troops and more to the graceful Vietnamese women gliding through the streets in their traditional *áo dài*—the long, flowing tunics that seemed to capture the elegance and resilience of their culture (Image: Vietnamese Woman).

My visit to Vietnam was brief but the country's atmosphere of uncertainty and transformation left a lasting impression. I would happily return to Vietnam in the years to come—under very different circumstances.

From Saigon, I flew to Manila, Philippines, a city that would later become deeply familiar to me. One of my strongest impressions then were the empty

streets of Makati, the government and financial district—a stark contrast to the Manila I would experience in the 1990s, when I actually lived there and found traffic congestion nearly unbearable.

While in Manila, I was advised to visit the famous *Pagsanjan Falls*, a natural wonder about 100 kilometers southeast of the city (Image: Pagsanjan Falls). I took a bus to Pagsanjan, where I hired a dugout canoe along with two boatmen. Their task was nothing short of extraordinary—they rowed against the rushing stream, and when boulders blocked our way, they hoisted the canoe (with me still inside) over the boulders and against the current. The journey was an adventure in itself, but the final reward was breathtaking: the Pagsanjan Falls, pouring into a deep, inviting pool. Without hesitation, I plunged into the cool waters, allowing the powerful torrent to crash over me before making the return journey.

Back in Manila, I visited the *Church of the Black Nazarene*, home to a life-sized statue of Christ carrying His cross. The wooden figure's dark complexion has given it the name "Black Nazarene," and it is revered by devout Filipinos who believe in its miraculous powers. One of Christ's legs extends beyond the altar, allowing believers to go behind it and kiss His foot, an act thought to bring healing and divine favor (Image: Black Nazarene).

By this point in my travels through Africa and Asia, I had witnessed count-

less religious rituals and practices—some deeply moving, others profoundly foreign to me. But as I watched the faithful Filipinos press their lips against the statue's worn, darkened foot, I found myself taken aback. I could not help but think: Never before have I seen such pagan-like practice that appeared utterly outlandish to me.

From Manila, I flew to Hong Kong, a city that captivated me from the moment I arrived. I spent several days wandering the bustling streets, exploring the endless maze of shops (Image: Kowloon), and marveling at the sea of skyscrapers that stretched into the horizon. One of my favorite experiences

was taking the boat to Hong Kong Island, where I walked up to the Peak and back, soaking in breathtaking views of the city below (Image: View from Hong Kong Island).

While looking from the shore of Kowloon Peninsula onto Hong Kong Island, I couldn't help but notice a towering new addition to the skyline: the Connaught Center (now called Jardine House). Standing at an impressive 178 meters, it was not only the tallest

building in Hong Kong but in all of Asia at the time. Its modern architecture made it glaringly conspicuous by the waterfront.

However, when I returned to Hong Kong twenty years later, I could hardly recognize the building amidst the forest of skyscrapers that had since risen around it. The Connaught Center, which had once been the tallest structure in Asia, now seemed small and completely overshadowed. Today, over 160 buildings exceed its height, with the International Commerce Center towering at 484 meters, more than double the size of the Connaught Center. In fact, Hong Kong now boasts more than 560 skyscrapers that rise to 150 meters or higher—a stark contrast to Frankfurt, for instance, which has only 20 buildings of that size. In any case, back when I first visited Hong Kong in 1973 and again when I returned with my family decades later, this city's incredible skyline and buzzling urban flurry was and will remain perhaps the most mindboggling metropolis of the world.

My final destination in Asia was Tokyo, a city that immediately made it clear that it was probably the most expensive place I had visited thus far. Given the steep costs and the fact that my round-the-world ticket, which was valid for only a year, was fast approaching its expiration date, I decided to limit my stay to just three days. Nonetheless, I had three things in mind which I wanted to experience in Japan: (1) explore this bustling metropolis, which was the world's most populous city at the time, (2) take a ride on the *Shinkansen*, the fastest train in the world, and (3) visit the iconic *Mount Fuji*.

On my first day, I wandered the vast expanse of Tokyo, absorbing the city's frenetic energy, its neon lights, and its harmonious blend of tradition and modernity (Image: Tokio), and I also visited one of the typical Japanese gardens (Image next page: Japanese Gar-den). The following day, I boarded the Shinkansen, or Bullet Train as it is also called, which lived up to its reputation for speed and efficiency (Image next page: Bullet Train). However, I chose only to travel to its first stop—the Shin-Fuji Station—where I transferred to a bus that would take me closer to Mount Fuji.

When I arrived there, however, I was disappointed to find the mountain completely obscured by a thick veil of clouds. The spectacular shape and snow-capped peak of Fuji-san were nowhere to be seen. I only briefly entertained the idea of climbing Mount Fuji—a journey that would take about 6-7 hours up and 3-5 hours down. But time was not on my side, and I wasn't exactly the most enthusiastic hiker. So, after spending a short while at the base of the mountain, I opted to return to the train station. Rather than purchasing another expensive Shinkansen ticket, I chose to board a normal train, which made frequent stops on the way back to Tokyo, offering a slower, but more affordable journey. The following day, I boarded my flight to my penultimate destination: Hawaii.

Upon arriving in Hawaii, I discovered something truly extraordinary: at Honolulu Airport, there were numerous faucets offering pineapple

juice—completely free of charge! It felt like an unexpected gift, a refreshing treat after a long journey. Hawaii is famous for its abundant pineapple plantations and canning companies, and the fruit has become one of the state's major exports.

I was picked up from the airport by a former fellow student from Pacific Union College, who had made Honolulu her home. We had been in touch before my trip, and she had graciously invited me to stay with her parents' home and explore the island together. Over the next few days, we toured some of the pineapple plantations and visited a pineapple canning factory, where I gained insight into the process that made Hawaii synonymous with this tropical fruit.

Of course, no trip to Hawaii would be complete without some time spent at the famous Waikiki Beach (Image: Kurt and Friend). We also made our way to the Halona Blowhole, a natural wonder near Waikiki. During high tide, ocean water is pushed through underground lava tubes, erupting through an opening in the ground to form an impressive geyser. However, when we visited, it was low tide, which gave us the rare opportunity to actually swim in the Blowhole itself. As the ocean waves surged, we were playfully pushed up and down in the water, creating a unique and altogether fun experience (Image: Blowhole).

At last, the time came to say farewell to my friend and begin the journey back to where this remarkable voyage around the world had first begun: to San Francisco. Along the way, I had explored many new countries across Africa and Asia, lived among some of the poorest communities I had ever

encountered, and witnessed both the natural and man-made wonders of the world. I returned with a deep sense of fulfillment, grateful for an experience that few are fortunate enough to have: the opportunity to meet and connect with people of diverse ethnicities and cultures around the world—encounters that deeply enriched my life and left me forever changed.

Back in the U.S.

The final flight on my round-the-world ticket took me from Honolulu back to San Francisco. I had not only reached the end of my journey but also the end of my financial means. When I had first set out from San Francisco, I had with me $1,000 in traveller's cheques which I could cash whenever needed. That sum was my lifeline, covering my accommodations and meals during the 2 ½ months of travel that had taken me across multiple continents. But by the time I landed in San Francisco, I had just $4 left. With that small amount, I paid for the bus ride back from the airport to my former college, where I had graduated only a year earlier.

Once back at the college after a three-hour bus ride, I began to look for a place to stay and for an opportunity to work, hoping to earn enough to carry on from there. I found a temporary gardening job, which allowed me to earn a bit of money. With those hard-earned dollars, I was able to fly to Los Angeles to visit my good old friend Ted Mamoulelis, who had married there the year before—I had been honored to serve as his best man. Now, Ted and his wife were living in Los Angeles, and I was eager to catch up with them after months of travel. After a few days with Ted, I flew back to San Francisco.

From San Francisco, I needed to make my way to Michigan to begin my Master's program. The most affordable option was to transfer a vehicle which its owner had driven to San Francisco but no longer wished to take back across the country. The arrangement was simple: drive the car back and pay only for gasoline. So, I teamed up with a female student from my college, and together we drove a station wagon from San Francisco to Chicago.

We drove nearly nonstop, taking turns behind the wheel, sharing the load as we crossed the vast American landscape. Our only stop was in Salt Lake City, the capital of Utah and the heart of the Mormon Church. Though we couldn't visit the Mormon Temple – as it was off-limits to non-Mormons – we did take the opportunity to explore the Salt Lake Tabernacle, just next to the temple. Known for its exceptional acoustics, it houses the famous Mormon Tabernacle Choir, which performs here regularly. The grandeur of the Tabernacle left a lasting impression, marking our brief yet memorable stop on the journey.

Upon our arrival in Chicago, we paused to get our bearings and figure out the best route to our final destination. I noticed that one of the tires was losing air. Naturally, I decided to change it, but when I went to the back of the car to check for the spare, I made a startling discovery: There was no spare tire. We had driven all the way from San Francisco to Chicago without one! Somehow, we had made it to Chicago safely, and now it was time to deliver the car. We drove it to the designated drop-off point and informed the recipient that they would need to get a spare tire quickly.

I said good bye to my good companion who went about her ways, and then reached out to my old friend and fellow student at PUC, Rudi Maier, who by now had already spent a year at Andrews University. He quickly came to pick me up and take me to Berrien Springs, Michigan. It was there that I would spend the next year working toward my Master of Arts degree in Theology/Religion, marking the next chapter of my academic journey.

I had received a scholarship to cover my tuition fees at Andrews University (Image: Andrews University), but I still had to work to cover my room and board. I found accommodation in a flat that I shared with a student from Denmark.

During my time at Andrews, I had the privilege of studying under several notable professors. One was Dr. Raoul Dederen from Belgium, who taught a course on Revelation and Inspiration. From him I learned the critical importance of understanding one's basic theological presuppositions. Dr. Hans LaRondelle from the Netherlands, a strong advocate for the justification through faith, also left a lasting impression; I later translated one of his books into German. Dr. Gottfried Oosterwal, again from the Netherlands, taught an excellent course on Cultural Anthropology, which provided the theoretical rationale to my experiences in Africa and Asia and taught me that one's way of thinking and living depends not so much on one's own conscious decisions and choices as it hinges on the mores and traditions of one's own culture and customs and ethnic standards that we adopt most often without even being aware of them.

Then there was Dr. Mervyn Maxwell, who taught history of the Seventh-day Adventist Church. While conservative, he was a kind and empathetic person. He must have noticed my inquisitive nature and critical mind, and expressed some concern regarding my orthodoxy. "I hope and fear for your future," he wrote under one of my papers. In hindsight, his fears were more than justified because in the long run I turned out to be a non-conformist Adventist and later even a Non-Adventist. Maxwell would have seen his worst expectations come true.

At Andrews, I also reconnected with Gerhard Hasel whom I had met years earlier in Tennessee. However, I did not take a course from him, as I felt he was too conservative for my taste. Instead, I enrolled in a course on Logic taught by a female professor whose name I can no longer recall. But I still remember how valuable that course was in reinforcing the idea that conclusions must be built on truthful premises. If premises are false, then the conclusion of the argument may be entirely logical and consistent, but not necessarily true. Hence, logical deductions are not enough to arrive at truth: You must also review your premises. It was a lesson that stuck with me and influenced my thinking in profound ways.

I completed my studies at Andrews University and earned my Master's degree. As my time in Berrien Springs came to a close, I attended a week-long conference on Biblical Hermeneutics. I noticed that all of the speakers had been chosen for their conservative theological positions, and those with

a more modern or critical approach to Biblical scholarship were conspicuously absent and not invited.

Curious and somewhat annoyed, I approached the organizer of the conference, a high-ranking representative of the Adventist Church leadership, and asked him why professors with a more liberal hermeneutical outlook on Biblical scholarship were not included in the program. He seemed caught off guard, unable to give a satisfactory answer. He looked at me as though I had just landed from another planet, and I left the conversation with a sense of frustration about the narrow scope of the event. I knew that for me, this wasn't yet the end of my journey to fully understand the Bible.

During my last weeks at Andrews, I became acquainted with the lovely daughter of one of the professors (Image: Kurt and Friend). We dated for a short time, but by that point, I had already decided to return to Germany to pursue post-graduate theological studies at the University of Tübingen. Saying goodbye to her was difficult, but I had my sights set on the next chapter of my life.

I boarded the plane to Frankfurt, marking the end of my American experience. Although I would make further brief visits to the U.S. during the following years, this American chapter of my life was coming to a close, and I was ready to continue my academic journey back in Europe.

Beautiful Tübingen

Upon arriving in Germany, I made my way to my parents' home, nestled at the far end of a modest village called Hertlingshausen, not far from Kaiserslautern (Picture: Kurt's Parents). I informed them of my desire to pursue further studies at the University of Tübingen, drawn by the esteemed reputation of its theology faculty.

Without much delay, I enrolled at the University of Tübingen and began attending various lectures and seminars. Though my ultimate aim was to earn a doctorate—be it a Ph.D. or a Doctor of Theology—my immediate focus was on immersing myself in the historical-critical method of biblical interpretation. I had encountered both praise and criticism of this approach and felt compelled to form my own opinion. Before rendering any judgment, I resolved to understand its various methods and foundational presuppositions. Thus, alongside my coursework, I undertook a personal inquiry into Historical Criticism—an intellectual journey that would soon upend many of my theological convictions.

Among the faculty, one figure made a mark in terms of biblical hermeneutics: Professor Peter Stuhlmacher. I had the privilege of attending his courses on the Epistle to the Romans and on Hermeneutics. Stuhlmacher was a distinguished New Testament scholar, gifted with the ability to speak in long, intricate sentences of such precision and clarity that they could have been transcribed directly to print. In his Hermeneutics course, he lamented the flood of speculative and often insufficiently substantiated hypotheses that supposedly pervaded much of New Testament scholarship. Yet, for all his criticism, he remained deeply committed to a rigorous, albeit judicious application of the historical-critical method.

I recall vividly a moment in his class when Stuhlmacher discussed the book *Das Ende der historisch-kritischen Methode* ("The End of the Historical Critical Method") by Gerhard Maier—who, as it happened, was seated behind me among the audience. Stuhlmacher addressed him directly, challenging Maier to reconsider the arguments of his book. Having read the work myself, I found it unpersuasive, though it had garnered considerable acclaim not only among fundamentalist readers but also within the conservative circles of the Lutheran Church.

Ironically, it was Maier who would go on to become Bishop of the Lutheran Church in the state of Württemberg. Meanwhile, the name of Peter Stuhlmacher, a towering figure in New Testament studies by comparison, has faded into relative obscurity.

Another professor who left a lasting impression on me was Eberhard Jüngel, a commanding figure in systematic theology and a thinker of remarkable depth and creativity. His lectures, attended by hundreds, were models of profundity and intellectual rigor, always meticulously prepared to cater to the needs of his students. I had the pleasure of taking his course entitled "Love – What Is It?," an experience that proved both intellectually rich and personally rewarding. Jüngel was the author of the seminal work *Gott als Geheimnis der Welt* ("God as Mystery of the World"), a profound exposition on the question of God—a text to which I have often returned in my own writings.

Equally memorable was Hartmut Gese, a distinguished Old Testament scholar whose course and seminar on the history of Israel I attended. Gese's scholarship opened my eyes to alternative geographical and historical understandings of biblical narratives. One particularly striking insight were his arguments that the mountain later referred to as Sinai (or Horeb) was not located in the Sinai Peninsula, as traditionally assumed, but rather in the northwestern region of Arabia. This provocative idea would later find its way into my own book, *Und sie dreht sich doch!*

In the realm of *textual criticism*, Professor Walter Thiele stood out as an exemplary scholar. His teachings illuminated the intricate and meticulous process by which the New Testament manuscripts had been transmitted and preserved over centuries. Under his instruction, I came to understand how textual variants are evaluated and how scholars reconstruct the standard text of Scripture from a wealth of available manuscript evidence or "readings."

While immersed in Thiele's course, I also engaged independently with other branches of the historical-critical method: literary criticism, tradition criticism, source criticism, form criticism, and redaction criticism. Contrary to the suspicions held by some, I came to see that none of these methods, when rightly applied, are inherently subversive or heretical. On the contrary, they serve to deepen one's understanding of the biblical text—its composition, development, and theological message. Just as the principles of textual criticism guide us in establishing the most reliable biblical text, so too do these related methodologies provide tools for discerning the layered and dynamic history of the Scriptures.

What became increasingly clear to me was that Historical Criticism is not a single, monolithic discipline but a collection of scholarly tools—tools which, like any instrument in the hands of a craftsman, require careful handling. The conclusions one draws from these methods depend not only on the data but also on the discretion and interpretive wisdom of the scholar. Overhasty judgments are seldom warranted; discernment and humility are indispensable companions on this path of inquiry.

Among the distinguished figures I encountered at Tübingen was Heiko Oberman, an eminent scholar of church history whose course on Erasmus of Rotterdam I had the pleasure of attending. A Dutchman by origin, Oberman had previously held a professorship at Harvard but chose to relocate to the University of Tübingen—not only drawn by the renown of its theological faculty, but also by the city itself, whose attractiveness is legendary (Image).

Tübingen, then as now, stands among the most enchanting towns in all of Germany and is perhaps – dare I say it? – the most beautiful of them all. With its charming half-timbered houses, vibrant marketplace, the ornate city hall, and its rich academic atmosphere, Tübingen possesses a timeless allure. It is a city where medieval architecture and intellectual life meet in harmonious resonance, making it not merely a place of study, but a place to enjoy life in general.

During my time there, I enrolled in a diverse array of further interesting courses: one on Pietism, another on the Gospel of Mark, yet another on Hinduism, and also a seminar on the Lausanne Movement, the latter taught by the staunchly conservative Professor Peter Beyerhaus, who unabashedly identified himself as an "evangelical."

My studies were not confined to theology alone; I also pursued Latin and Hebrew, fulfilling the requirements for the *Latinum* and *Hebraicum*, the official certifications of linguistic proficiency in Germany (in addition to the Greek I had studied at PUC). Despite my own sense of unreadiness, I passed the Hebrew examination with the highest distinction.

Seated beside me in that Latin class was a striking young woman who, after our final lecture, offered to accompany me to the train station—my home being in the nearby village of Kusterdingen, a suburb of Tübingen. Her unexpected interest led to a brief but memorable romantic and intimate interlude. Eventually, she returned to the United States, where she had previously lived—and, as I would later learn, where another companion awaited her return.

Throughout my time in Tübingen, I remained actively involved with the local Seventh-day Adventist Church. I preached regularly, offering sermons that sought to bridge traditional faith with emerging insight, and I also engaged in youth ministry. Parallel to this ecclesial commitment, I continued my personal and academic exploration of Historical Criticism—a journey that profoundly expanded my theological horizon.

What had begun as an introduction to scholarly methodology deepened into a broader reflection on the assumptions that undergird our entire reading of Scripture. At Andrews University, I had already come to understand the importance of foundational premises in theological thought. Now, in Tübingen, I was compelled to confront the hermeneutical presuppositions that underpin our interpretation of the Bible itself.

Among the questions that captivated me was the origin and formation of the Biblical canon. Why, I asked, were certain texts included in what we call the "Bible," while others were excluded? And why did Martin Luther remove some books from the Lutheran canon—books that to this day remain part of the Catholic Bible? Who, ultimately, decided what belonged within the sacred scripture and what did not? And by what criteria were such decisions made?

To seek answers, I also turned to the non-canonical literature of the first century—gospels and letters that, while excluded from the official canon, offered revealing glimpses into the diversity and creativity of early Christian writings. Some of these pseudepigraphical texts were edifying, others extravagant—embellished to such an extent that they bordered on the absurd. Yet even these excesses were instructive. They illuminated the imaginative ways in which early religious communities shaped their narratives and embellished their oral traditions.

This, in turn, led me to reconsider the biblical texts themselves. How much of what is recorded reflects actual historical events, and how much of it is the product of theological storytelling, shaped and reshaped in the crucible of oral tradition?

I came to believe that a distinction ought to be made between what I called "historical factuality" and "theological truth." Not every detail in Scripture can or should be regarded as a literal historical account. Rather, the deeper purpose of the Bible is to convey theological meaning: insights into the human nature, into the mystery of existence, into the relationship between the human and the divine.

The Bible does not pretend to be a scientific textbook for historians, biologists, geologists, or astronomers. Its truth lies elsewhere—in the spiritual and existential questions it dares to pose, and in the responses it offers. In wrestling with these realizations, I slowly came to see that I was about to undergo a profound transformation. Where once I had stood firmly within the framework of a fundamentalist evangelical worldview, I now found myself drawn to the posture of a modern liberal theologian. This required a thorough rethinking of nearly every classical Christian doctrine—Christology, soteriology, eschatology, the doctrine of humanity, and even the nature of God. I had come to recognize that hermeneutics—the art and science of interpretation—is the foundation upon which all theology is built.

In terms of Christology, I began to doubt not only the virgin birth of Jesus, which I had previously believed, but also the physical resurrection of Christ and his presumed divine sonship. I came to realize that when Jesus spoke of God as "his Father," he meant this in a metaphorical rather than an ontological sense. Within Judaism, divine sonship was a figurative way of expressing closeness to God.

The virgin birth, I concluded, served merely as an outward sign of that close relationship (or "sonship") between Jesus and "his Father" in heaven. Only the Gospels of Matthew and Luke report the virgin birth, while Mark and John appear not to have known of it. Even the Apostle Paul never mentions it. Instead, he connects Christ's sonship with the resurrection rather than with his birth. And had he known of the virgin birth, I thought, he surely would have referred to it.

I also began to question the bodily resurrection of Christ. Although Paul firmly believed in it, he indicated that the resurrected body differed entirely from the earthly body: "It is sown a natural body; it is raised a spiritual body" (1 Cor. 15:44). I came to believe that Christ's resurrection should be interpreted not in physical terms, but in spiritual terms. To insist on a bodily resurrection places undue emphasis on historical factuality rather than on the theological truth the event conveys. A physical interpretation stresses a mere miracle, whereas a spiritual interpretation allows Christ to live within us and enables us to live in him as his followers.

Other traditional beliefs also became uncertain for me, particularly the eschatological expectations emphasized by the Adventist Church, which claimed to know many of the events that would precede the end of the world. The Adventists originated from the belief that Christ would return to earth in 1844. As is well known, he did not come at that time — nor during the century that followed. Would he ever return? And would there be life after death? I asked myself. If not, would that be a tragedy? How would I feel if there were no afterlife at all? I came to realize that such a prospect would be quite acceptable for me; I no longer felt a need for an afterlife.

And what about God? Naturally, if traditional Christology was a product of human imagination, perhaps God was as well. Serious doubts arose in me about the existence of God. Still, I chose not to pursue those doubts further and decided to leave the question for another time.

In any case, the more I studied theology, the more I felt the need to distinguish between "historical factuality," which cannot be established for many historical, geological, or astronomical references in the Bible, and the Bible's "theological truths," which it is the theologian's task to ascertain and expound it.

During this time I also began to become interested in scientific questions, especially regarding the relationship between religion and the natural sciences. I can hardly count the workshops and conferences I attended over the years which dealt with such topics as astronomy, geology, biological evolution, mind and body etc. Already at Pacific Union College I had taken courses in astronomy, biology and geology, but now my interest in these subjects deepened, especially as they related to our general world view and how they influence our religious and theological thinking. The relationship between theology and the natural sciences has become somewhat of an expertise of mine.

During this same period, my intellectual world broadened yet further through encounters with psychology. A friend of mine, a social educator by training, had begun organizing group therapy sessions and invited me to participate in one of them. I joined out of curiosity and quickly found the experience enriching, even therapeutic. As time went on, he asked if I would help co-lead some of his groups, and I agreed. They gave me the opportunity to not only understand myself better, but to also appreciate the inherent reasons why people become what they are (something that was further deepened when I also participated in so-called "family constellation" workshops in later years).

At one of these early group sessions, a young and striking woman—already married—was among the participants. Weeks later, she appeared at my door unannounced, seeking nothing more than to spend the night with me. I did not turn her away. It would not be the last time I found myself the unexpected recipient of such attention—occasions I did not resist, but accepted, with the complex mixture of curiosity, desire, and humanity that marked this chapter of my life.

With the modest foundation in psychology I had acquired by that point, I felt prepared to volunteer for what is known in German as "Telefonseelsorge"—a crisis telephone hotline where individuals facing personal turmoil could call, anonymously, to speak with someone willing to listen and perhaps offer a word of guidance or reassurance.

At the time, there were no rigid requirements to become a telephone counselor. There existed neither a formal certification process nor a handbook on how to prepare for such delicate conversations. It was only later that the theologian and psychotherapist Professor Dr. Helmut Harsch developed his now-classic work *Theory and Practice of Telephone Counseling*, which would go on to become the standard text in the field—a prerequisite for anyone wishing to serve in such a capacity. I had the privilege of getting to know Helmut Harsch much later in life, and our acquaintance blossomed into a short, albeit deep and enduring friendship. But during my early days in Tübingen, his thoughtful primer was not yet available.

Instead, my suitability for the task was assessed through a personal interview with a psychologist who practiced in Tübingen. During our conversation, she posed many questions, among them this one: Did my apparent self-confidence come naturally, or had I consciously cultivated it? Without hesitation, I admitted that it was the result of deliberate effort—a demeanor I had practiced and refined over time. She smiled, seemingly pleased by my candor, and approved me for the role.

And so I began serving as a telephone counselor, entering the quiet, often poignant world of anonymous confidences—a world in which the simple act of listening could become an act of compassion. Through the counseling experience, I came to understand that the troubles weighing on the clients were selddom resolved by clever advice from the counselor, but rather by uncovering the solutions that quietly lay dormant within the clients themselves.

Of all the theology faculty at the University of Tübingen, the one most renowned internationally—particularly in the United States—was Jürgen Moltmann. His seminal work *Theology of Hope* had achieved global acclaim and positioned him as a central voice in contemporary theology. I attended his course on Christology as well as a seminar exploring mysticism. It was during this seminar that I approached Moltmann with the hope that he might serve as the supervisor for my doctoral work. He responded favorably but asked that I first submit a paper on a topic related to mysticism.

I chose to write on Hildegard of Bingen—a 12th-century Benedictine abbess, mystic, and visionary, who was also a prolific writer, composer, and thinker. My fascination with Hildegard arose, in part, from the intriguing parallels I perceived between her and Ellen G. White, the Adventist prophetess and mystic who, too, had emerged as a powerful voice in both religious writing and ecclesiastical leadership. Upon reviewing my paper, Moltmann agreed to take me on as a doctoral candidate, and we began discussing potential topics for my dissertation. My favorite topic was "visions" and "sight" in the Bible. Moltmann feared that this theme might be too extensive to be completed in three years.

Regrettably, the doctoral project I had hoped to undertake under Moltmann's supervision never came to fruition. There were several reasons for this unfortunate turn of events.

First and foremost, I found myself in financial constraints and had no choice but to begin working in order to support myself. What had been intended as a period of academic immersion was overtaken by the practical demands of livelihood. So I looked for some income-generating activities. In one case, I had contacts with an entrepreneur who wanted to establish a relationship with a businessman from the United Arab Emirates and asked me to visit him. I flew to Abu Dabhi only to find out that the Arab businessman was not really offering the opportunity we had hoped for. I spent a couple of nights in a posh hotel, only to return to Germany empty-handed. I had to look for another job.

Secondly—and more gravely—I was confronted by a serious health issue. During a comprehensive medical examination, a tumor was discovered on my pituitary gland, located deep in the very center of my skull. The diagnosis led to two separate surgical interventions: the first performed at the University Hospital in Frankfurt/Main, and the second at the renowned University Hospital Grosshadern in Munich. The second procedure became necessary as there still was a residual of the tumor that, if not removed, could have posed a threat to the optic nerve.

During the preliminary examinations, I underwent, among other things, a pneumoencephalography, a diagnostic radiology that produced X-ray films of the head after air was injected into the brain. The method has since been replaced by computerized technologies as it was a painful and sometimes dangerous procedure. I cannot remember anything more sickening and nauseating than this pneumoencephalography, and I vomited during the procedure, as I had hardly ever done before or after. As it turned out, this type of diagnosis wasn't even necessary for the surgery that followed.

Both operations were conducted transsphenoidally—that is, by navigating through the nasal cavity and carefully cutting through the bone surrounding the sphenoid sinus. Each surgery required the combined expertise of an ENT surgeon and a neurosurgeon. Following the excision of the tumor, the void left in the sinus bone had to be reconstructed—during the first surgery with the very bone fragments that had been removed, and during the second operation with a graft fashioned from a strip of tendon taken from my right thigh.

I recall an amusing moment when some years later a physician noticed the scar on my thigh and asked about its origin. "I had surgery on my pituitary gland," I replied. He looked at me with a mixture of curiosity and disbelief. "Then you must be an anatomical miracle," he said, laughing. I joined in his laughter and explained the intricate pathway of the operation.

In any case, while the first surgery was only moderately successful, the second was executed with perfect precision, and I have enjoyed full health ever since. For that, I remain deeply grateful.

The third reason I did not pursue the dissertation was more personal and joyful: I met Aline, the woman who would turn out to be my wife. She introduced an entirely new chapter to my life—one marked not by scholarly ambition alone, but by love, companionship, and the unfolding of a shared journey. Aline was intelligent and eloquent, with a pretty face and a perfect figure. I quickly became addicted to her.

These were sufficient reasons for me to set aside, for the time being at least, this project of a doctoral study. I have sometimes regretted not having pursued this any more, as a doctorate would probably have opened up more possibilities in terms of my professional career.

The beautiful town of Tübingen was, in many respects, an important turning point in my life. It was a place of intellectual expansion, theological transformation, medical healing and personal growth. But more than anything else, it was there—amid lectures and libraries, church pews and quiet conversations—that I got to know the woman who would become my wife, Aline.

Aline

While still enrolled as a student in Tübingen, I decided to invest in a new IBM typewriter with a typeball—then considered the pinnacle of technological advancement. Shortly thereafter, I stumbled across a small newspaper advertisement seeking someone to type manuscripts. Thinking it might promise a modest source of income, I responded to the ad.

The woman who had placed the ad introduced herself as Aline. She came by to deliver the first manuscript—an ordinary gesture, yet one that marked the beginning of something far from ordinary. I was immediately struck by

her presence: a graceful figure, soft dark eyes, hair to match, and a gentle, almost childlike voice. There was a kindness and calm in her demeanor, an elegance not only in her appearance but in her manner of being. She told me she earned her living typing dissertations and book manuscripts, back when typewriters—not computers—were the indispensable tools of the trade.

After a couple of visits with this lady, I found myself confiding to my mother that I had met a beautiful young woman whom I could imagine marrying. There was an empathy in her that disarmed me, and an inner strength that quietly drew me in. I soon learned that Aline had a two-year-old son, a bright and endearing boy whom I liked almost instantly. The bond between them only deepened my admiration. In my eyes, Aline seemed to embody everything I had ever hoped for in a partner: she was articulate, emotionally attuned, gracious, devoted, and beautiful (Images: Aline).

Eventually, I expressed my interest more directly, and before long we began a relationship that quickly grew in both intensity and seriousness. Only a couple of weeks into our relationship and emboldened by affection, I hinted that I could imagine proposing to her. Yet I held back from a formal proposal, as we barely knew each other and as I was burdened by the knowledge of not yet being in a financial position to fully support a marriage. The next day, however, Aline brought it up herself, asking whether my words had, in fact, been intended as a proposal. I explained honestly that while I could not yet offer her the material stability I wished to, my intention to marry her was sincere. She seemed pleased by this, and soon we began to make tentative preparations for a life together. As things progressed, she invited me to give up my own flat and move into her spacious, elegantly furnished apartment.

But I had yet to discover another side of Aline—one that was passionate, yes, but also intensely emotional. Her love, when given, was deep and loyal. But her sensitivities ran equally deep, and when wounded, she could lash out with a sharpness that startled and injured me. I, for my part, responded with a practiced exterior coolness—an armor that concealed the fact that I, too, was often hurt. It was a dance of emotional misalignment: Where I sought to contain, she sought to express; where she surged, I receded.

As with many inexperienced couples, small misunderstandings began to spiral. A careless word, an unresolved tension, a moment of silence misread as indifference—these grew into conflict. One disagreement begot another, one wound opened yet more. Eventually, in a moment of anger and disillusionment, Aline demanded that I move out.

What had seemed like a serendipitous gift—a meeting shaped by chance and filled with promise—dissolved much too quickly into heartbreak. What I had believed to be the beginning of a shared destiny now appeared, with painful clarity, as a mistake. A misstep not just in love, but in judgment. And so it ended, not with a vow, but with a departure. A lesson carved into the still-soft clay of youth and longing.

By that time, I had realized it was imperative to find gainful employment, and so I responded to a job advertisement posted by a development agency. To my surprise and relief, I was invited for an interview and was soon offered a position with the Christian Blind Mission (known as *Christoffel-Blindenmission* in German, or CBM), an organization devoted to aiding the blind and disabled, and supporting programs for the prevention and treatment of blindness. Their headquarters were located in Bensheim, not far from Frankfurt/Main. And so, I left the familiar comforts of Tübingen behind and moved to a region known as the Odenwald, some two hundred kilometers to the north, to begin this new chapter of my life.

At that point, I had no occasion to inform Aline of my whereabouts. I assumed—painfully, but with resignation—that our separation was final. I settled into my new environment and sought to focus on my work. Then, after several months had passed, the unexpected happened: I received a phone call from Aline. Her voice on the line was at once familiar and tentative. She told me she wished to come and see me—there was something, she said, she needed to "find out." Somewhat stunned, yet inwardly stirred, I agreed.

A few days later, she arrived. I welcomed her into my modest apartment, and we went out for dinner. I can recall barely being able to eat, my appetite lost in the nervous anticipation of what the evening might hold. What would she say? What did she feel? What did I still feel?

Over the course of the evening, Aline opened her heart. She admitted to regret how she had treated me, and that she believed we should give our relationship a second chance. I listened quietly, and then told her with measured honesty that I was indeed open to a new beginning—but only if we could ensure that the painful emotional patterns of the past would not return. I could not endure the same wounds again.

She agreed, and from that point onward, we found our way back to one another—though still separated by distance. I made frequent drives down to Tübingen, while she, in turn, visited me in the Odenwald. Those were times of rediscovery—lighter, more thoughtful, and tender in ways we had

not managed before. I recall with special fondness one visit when she brought along her son, Patrick. We ventured out for a long hike through the forest, the three of us wrapped in the simplicity of shared time and nature's quietude.

But as we neared the end of our walk, a sudden and biting rainstorm swept in from the hills. We were drenched—soaked through to the bone by the cold and unrelenting downpour. Laughing and shivering, we hurried back to my flat, dripping wet and thoroughly chilled. There, we peeled off our soggy clothes and, without a second thought, the three of us slipped into a warm bathtub. The water embraced us with comfort, and for a while we simply lay there—together, safe, and warm—as if the storm had washed away the residue of past grief and left only the fragile promise of renewal (Image: Kurt and Aline).

We were married on the 27th of August, 1982, in the historic town hall of Tübingen (Image: Tübingen Townhall). The ceremony was a modest civil affair, attended by Aline's son Patrick, her mother, her brother Manfred, and my close friend Wolfgang Alberth. We had decided against a church wedding for by then I had grown quite distant from the Seventh-day Adventist Church, and Aline was not affiliated with any denomination at all. It was a simple, personal event, with only a small but meaningful ritual. Aline adopted my last name and made sure Patrick also took my name (Image: Kurt and Patrick). However, it was only when Patrick was about 35 that he requested me to officially adopt him as my son.

With marriage came the decision to begin a new chapter together, which for Aline meant leaving behind her spacious flat and the beautiful city of Tübingen. She was willing to make that sacrifice, and we began to search for a home closer to my new workplace at the Christian Blind Mission. We eventually rented a house in Lorsch, a small, historically significant town that became our new home.

Lorsch was best known for its "Königshalle," or King's Hall, a curious Carolingian structure that for a long time was believed to have been erected in honor of Charlemagne, who was said to have visited the region on several occasions. More recent archaeological research, however, suggests that the building may have been constructed closer to the year 900 A.D.—still ancient, still remarkable. The King's Hall was part of a powerful Benedictine monastery founded in 764 A.D., a center of learning and spiritual

influence whose possessions stretched from northern Germany all the way to the Vatican (Image: Aline, Kurt and Patrick before the King's Hall).

Apart from this storied legacy, however, Lorsch was a rather unremarkable place—especially when compared to the vibrant, intellectual atmosphere of Tübingen. Aline, who had grown fond of the lively streets and stimulating culture of university life, found it difficult to adjust. She once remarked, with a wry smile, "Having adapted to Lorsch, I could now go to almost anywhere in the world." Well, she never really adapted to this city.

Still, we made the best of our time there. Summers offered moments of escape, and we spent many of our vacations in the sun-kissed landscapes of Spain—Mallorca, Ibiza, Andalucía, and Murcia—where the warmth of the Mediterranean seemed to ease the weight of the mundane. We also explored farther afield: Israel, with its layered history and spiritual intensity, and Istanbul, where East and West seemed to converge in a tapestry of culture and memory.

Among the most unforgettable journeys our family ever embarked upon was a pilgrimage to Jordan—a land where history breathes through stone. We wandered through the majestic ruins of Jerash, stood in awe within the Roman amphitheater of Amman, and, at last, found ourselves in Petra—the ancient city carved into the soul of the earth (Images).

Petra, a 2000-year-old marvel, revealed to us its soaring temples, ornate royal tombs, Roman-style theaters, burial chambers, and solemn funeral

halls—each etched with time into the rose-red sandstone. It is a city not merely built, but summoned from the rock itself—a silent testament to the grandeur of human imagination and the passage of the Nabatean civilization. These sacred remnants, shaped by hands long vanished, left not only their image in our eyes but their echo in our hearts—an indelible impression, as if time itself had whispered to us through stone.

The relationship with Aline was deeply rewarding. I was in love, and so was she. We shared our lives together, got to know each other better, had our quarrels and differences, but on the whole lived happy lives with another. I also established a good relationship with Patrick. I had learned from Aline not to engage in any form of corporal punishment, and when problems arose, we always spoke about them, considering everybody's perspectives.

Apart from our private journeys, my new job also led me to travel on behalf CBM—trips that further broadened my view of the world. But no matter how far I journeyed, it was the shared life with Aline and Patrick that became the steady heartbeat of those years.

Christian Blind Mission (CBM)

The Christian Blind Mission had its origins in the vision and commitment of one man: Reverend Ernst J. Christoffel (1876–1955) from the German city of

Rheydt—now part of Mönchengladbach, which happens to be my birthplace. Christoffel was driven by a deep calling to serve the blind and disabled in poor countries. When he found no German missionary organization willing to send him abroad for such a purpose, he set out on his own, undeterred by the lack of institutional support (Image: Ernst J. Christoffel).

He went to Turkey and established a home for blind and disabled children in Malatya—an act of remarkable compassion and foresight at a time when such individuals were often hidden from society. Later, in Isfahan, Iran, he opened a school for the blind that continued to operate until the Islamic Revolution of 1979. In order to raise donations for the school in Germany, he founded a small not-for-profit organization.

When Christoffel passed away in Isfahan in 1955, it might have seemed like the end of his small society, had it not been for Pastor Siegfried Wiesinger who in 1961 was appointed to lead the fragile organization. Under his dynamic leadership, the once-modest NGO was transformed into one of the largest donor-funded development agencies in Germany (Image: Siegfried Wiesinger). Wiesinger was a fund-

raising genius, with a talent for storytelling, emotional connection, and a strategic mind for outreach. He cultivated a vast network of supporters—over 600,000 donors, who regularly received CBM's bimonthly donor magazine, a publication for which I held partial editorial responsibility for some time.

CBM's donors, many of whom contributed only small sums, collectively empowered the organization to fund development initiatives around the globe—amounting to $70 million or more annually at the time. The projects supported by CBM spanned a wide spectrum: medical missions to cure and prevent blindness, schools for the blind, education centers for the deaf, rehabilitation centers for the physically disabled, and institutions for those with intellectual challenges. It was a multifaceted response to some of the world's most neglected people.

Wiesinger himself was a visionary and fiercely committed leader, known for both his brilliance and his temperament. He read almost every letter donors sent to CBM and made sure that each received a personal reply—a testament to his belief in the value of every single donor. But his hot temper also made him a difficult figure at times. He could be uncompromising, and not all staff found him easy to work with. I myself (Image) had my severe disagreements with him, but our relationship evolved over time, and eventually he entrusted me with the responsibility for overseeing projects in West and East Asia—a role that would deeply shape the next stage of my professional life. For the projects in West Asia, we had no regional director stationed in the field, and so it became my responsibility to personally visit the region and get to know the programs we were supporting there.

In contrast, for East Asia we had a regional director located in Malaysia, but my team and I at headquarters were still tasked with ensuring that all financial statements submitted by Asian projects were in proper order, that progress reports were regularly submitted, and that the funds granted were being used in accordance with their designated purposes. I had three competent assistants who handled much of the day-to-day operations, but it fell to me to draft and sign important correspondence—sometimes addressed to as many as a hundred different project partners.

Travel became an integral part of my role. I visited projects in *TURKEY*, primarily in Istanbul and Ankara, where we had supported programs that catered to the needs of blind and disabled children. I also journeyed to *ISRAEL*, including visits to the *WEST BANK* and the *GAZA STRIP*. In Gaza, I witnessed a cataract surgery being performed—an impressive experience, particularly given the challenging conditions under which such procedures were carried out. During that same trip, I had the opportunity to explore the old city of Jerusalem, a place so filled with layered history and spiritual meaning that I immediately knew I had to return—next time, with Aline. And when we did, we also visited places like Acre, Haifa and Nazareth in the North of the country, Bethlehem and Jericho (or what was left of it) in the central region, and Masada and Aqaba in the South. Of course, we also took an obligatory swim in the Dead Sea.

My professional travels also brought me again to *JORDAN*, where I evaluated projects CBM was supporting, and then to *SYRIA*. In Damascus, I wandered through the immense and bustling central market inside the ancient city walls where I bought a Syrian lamp that still hangs over my dining table today. Adjacent to the central market stood the *Great Umayyad Mosque*, one of the oldest and largest mosques in the world. According to traditions dating back to the sixth century, it is believed to be the burial place of *John the Baptist*. Interestingly, this grand structure was once a Christian cathedral and the seat of the Patriarch of Antioch, until it was converted into a mosque during the Umayyad dynasty.

From Damascus, I continued north to *Aleppo*, a town with a rich history that dates back millennia—once Syria's largest city, before being surpassed by Damascus. In Aleppo, I visited an Armenian ophthalmologist whose eye clinic was supported by CBM. It was humbling to witness the work being done under modest conditions and yet with much dedication. Years later, when Aleppo was devastated by bombings during the Syrian conflict, I often thought of that visit—of the people I met, and of the fragile beauty of a city so deeply scarred by war.

One of the more unusual and adventurous trips I undertook was in 1985, when I accompanied my direct superior, the director of the overseas department, on a journey that took us to **LEBANON, PAKISTAN**, and **AFGHANISTAN**. Since the *Lebanese Civil War* was still raging at the time, flying directly into Beirut was not an option. Instead, we flew to Cyprus and from there took a ferry across the Mediterranean to Lebanon.

Upon arrival, we realized we had overlooked a small but critical detail: we hadn't obtained Lebanese visas in advance, mistakenly assuming that our German passports would grant us automatic entry. That assumption proved incorrect. Fortunately, the local project representative who had come to meet us was resourceful enough to arrange for our visas within just a few hours, and we were able to proceed with our visits to CBM-supported initiatives in Lebanon (Image: Kurt, Gerhard Weiland and a Lebanese Blind).

When asked where we were heading after our visit to Lebanon, we replied: "Afghanistan." Given that another war was raging there, too, at the time, the typical response was: "Well, hope you'll be safe."

Interestingly, when we finally arrived in Afghanistan and people asked us where we had come from, we answered: "From Lebanon." Their reaction, in light of the ongoing Lebanese Civil War, was: "Well, you can be lucky to have safely departed from there." We couldn't help but find that amusing— danger and instability had become the backdrop of our itinerary, and our journey seemed to be a constant trade-off between conflict zones. But people living in these places, often underestimated their own risks and overestimated those further away.

 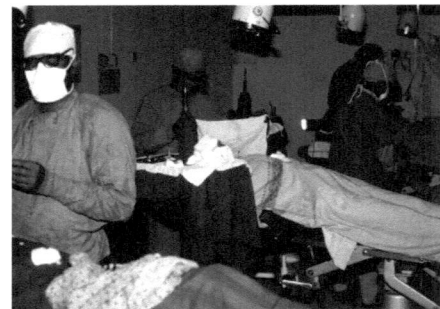

After finishing our visit to Lebanon, we took the ferry back to Cyprus and boarded a flight to Pakistan. Among the various CBM-supported projects we visited there, one in particular stood out: the Christian Taxila Eye Hospital, located near Islamabad. There we had the privilege of meeting its director, Dr. Norval Christy, a Harvard-educated ophthalmologist and a dedicated Christian who had committed most of his professional life to serving the blind in Pakistan.

Dr. Christy invited us into his operating theatre where we joined him during a cataract surgery session that had already started at 5 o'clock in the morning. The theatre had four operating tables placed side by side (Image previous page), and Dr. Christy moved from one to the next in rapid succession, performing one cataract surgery after another. His team took care of the pre-operative and post-operative procedures, allowing him to focus solely on the surgical task itself. In this way, he was able to restore sight to an astonishing 30 to 50 blind patients a day.

Back then, many Pakistanis still believed that losing one's sight was simply a part of growing old—something irreversible and to be accepted with resignation. They did not know that cataract blindness could be prevented, and many had gone completely blind – until finding out that there was a place where they could be made to see again. Dr. Christy's work had changed that old perception entirely. Word began to spread, even into remote areas, that

blindness was curable, and that there was real hope for those who had once believed themselves condemned to darkness (Image: Pakistani Blind).

At that time, the surgery was straightforward: the clouded lens was removed and later compensated with thick corrective glasses that, while bulky, allowed patients to regain a functional level of sight. Through decades of tireless work, Dr. Christy performed cataract surgeries on far more than 100,000 patients, the majority of whom had been living in near-total blindness. To get around, they had to be accompanied by a seeing relative, but now they could see again after their treatment at the Taxila hospital. Once provided with glasses, their faces were happily shining thanks to the life-changing operation. There was still a life with sight ahead of them.

We also visited the refugee camps near Peshawar, where tens of thousands of Afghan refugees had fled from the intense fighting between the Afghan *Mujahideen* and the Soviet forces. CBM was supporting several of the educational and rehabilitative initiatives being carried out in these camps. The scene there was both sobering and overwhelming—makeshift shelters stretched across dusty plains, filled with families who had lost everything yet clung to hope. The children were receiving basic education and rehabilitation support thanks to the collaboration between CBM and its local partners (Image: Afghan Refugees).

The Soviet invasion of Afghanistan in 1979 was a geopolitical move intended to pull the country into the Soviet sphere of influence by installing a puppet regime. While the Soviets attempted some modernization—such as improving infrastructure and introducing education for girls—the invasion itself was widely condemned and opposed. In response, countries including Pakistan, the U.S., the U.K., Iran, and China supported the Mujahideen resistance, which framed its fight as both a war of liberation and a defense of Islamic tradition.

The toll of this conflict was staggering, however: millions of Afghans were either killed or displaced, entire villages were reduced to rubble, and the social fabric of the nation was severely damaged. On the Soviet side, the war drained resources and morale. When Mikhail Gorbachev rose to power in Moscow, he eventually acknowledged the immense costs of the war and declared the beginning of the Soviet withdrawal, which took place between

1988 and 1989. Many historians have argued that the war in Afghanistan was instrumental in hastening the dissolution of the Soviet Union in 1991.

But during our visit to Afghanistan in 1985, the war was still in full force. The flight to Kabul offered a stark reminder of that: Our plane had to stay at a high cruising altitude before quickly circling and descending over the capital—a maneuver designed to reduce the risk of being hit by one of the Mujahideen's surface-to-air missiles.

After safely landing at Kabul International Airport, we proceeded to visit the NOOR Eye Hospital, which was operated by the *International Assistance Mission* (IAM) and funded in part by CBM. The hospital played a critical role in both curing and preventing blindness across Afghanistan, often serving patients from the most remote and underserved areas. We saw firsthand the quiet heroism of the staff who worked under great pressure and with minimal resources, yet delivered exceptional care with compassion.

The importance of the hospital could hardly be overstated. On a previous visit to Kabul by CBM director Siegfried Wiesinger, he had not only inspected the hospital but also paid a visit to the Afghan Ministry of Health. During the meeting, officials expressed gratitude for CBM's ongoing support but raised a pointed question: Why did CBM and IAM consistently send *Christian* doctors and staff to Afghanistan? Why not *Muslims*?

Wiesinger, never one to shy away from difficult conversations, answered candidly: *"It is difficult to find non-Christian staff who are willing to go to such under-developed places as Afghanistan. But Christians, following their Master, have the commitment and willingness to endure hardship and deprivation for the privilege of saving lives and preventing blindness."* His response may not have solved the underlying tension, but it was honest, and it highlighted the deeper conviction that drove so many of CBM's workers to the field.

On another trip to **PAKISTAN** in 1988, I was accompanied by a German ophthalmologist. Our task was to visit a range of eye hospitals and oph-

thalmic departments throughout the country in order to evaluate the support CBM had been providing, assess the quality of services, and identify both deficits and opportunities for future improvement. We traveled extensively—our itinerary included Lahore, Peshawar, Abbottabad, Sialkot, Quetta, Karachi, Hyderabad and other cities, each with its own unique challeng-

es and potentials. As always, it was not just the institutions that impressed us but the people – their uniqueness, their friendliness, their hospitality, their unwavering resilience (Image: Two Men Smoking).

One of our most significant visits was to the Civil Hospital in Karachi, where we encountered the inspiring legacy of Dr. Ruth Pfau. A German-born Catholic nun and medical doctor, Dr. Pfau had become something of a legend in Pakistan due to her tireless work among leprosy patients. She had established a treatment center and was instrumental in introducing "multidrug therapy," which not only halted the disease but also prevented the development of drug resistance.

When we later met Dr. Pfau in a remote corner of Baluchistan, she was attending to her rural patients with the same humble intensity. I recall her telling us, *"The leprosy patients look so good now that we have begun concentrating more on the cure of eye patients."* Her approach was both practical and visionary—adapting her medical priorities to meet the evolving needs of the communities she served. It was a powerful moment to witness such dedication.

We were deeply impressed not only by Dr. Pfau's medical expertise but by the quiet conviction with which she lived her mission. When asked why she had forgone the amenities and comforts of a Western lifestyle to dedicate her entire life to the people of Pakistan, her answer was simple and deeply moving: *"If I cannot alleviate the poverty of these people, at least I want to share in their poverty."*

It wasn't said with drama or self-pity—only a calm clarity that revealed how seriously she took her calling. Her presence had an almost magnetic serenity, and her words stayed with me long after we parted ways. In a world where many seek to elevate themselves above others, she had chosen solidarity over status, and service over comfort.

Our visits weren't limited to large urban hospitals. One of the more remarkable programs we evaluated was a mobile eye clinic—essentially a fully equipped operating theatre built into a truck that could navigate into the most remote and underserved regions of Pakistan. There, it would offer cataract surgeries and other treatments to people who otherwise would have no access to medical care. The concept was brilliant in its simplicity: bring the hospital to the patients, instead of asking the patients to find their way to a hospital.

During our extended travels, we quickly became accustomed to the way women dressed in public. In most areas of Pakistan, women wore a *Hijab* or *Chador*, covering their heads and often their faces, leaving only the eyes visible. In places like Afghanistan and Peshawar, even the eyes were concealed by the *Burka*, which had a fine mesh screen through which women could see, but through which no one could see them, not even their eyes. It was a culture in which visual privacy was held in high regard, and for days on end, we rarely saw a woman's face.

That is why our visit to a girls' boarding school run by Catholic Sisters in Karachi left such a strong impression on us. The Sisters, who had been working in the region for years, invited us to tour the school, including the dormitories. And there they were—some thirty or more teenage girls, perhaps 15 to 17 years old, dressed informally and not wearing any scarves or hijabs. Their uncovered faces, lit up by laughter and curiosity, left us momentarily speechless. It was a simple thing—young girls in a safe environment, smiling and talking freely—but for us, after so many days in conservative settings, it was both unexpected and deeply delightful. We were struck by their natural beauty, of course, but more than that, by the sense of normalcy and freedom these young students exuded in that setting. It reminded us that behind the veils and cultural norms, the same youthful spirit and dreams lived in every corner of the world.

Back in Germany, I pursued my work at CBM's Asia Desk. But I also had to attend to my private life. By some coincidence, I met a young lady who wanted to create a theatre group and was looking for voluntary actors. I offered my services, quite confident that I would be a good actor. She invited me to participate, and I got a role in "Charley's Aunt," a humoresque play that we performed for a number of months at a Bensheim theatre (Image:

Kurt as Actor). I also played another role in a different play the following year.

Unfortunately, one evening as I was driving home from work—it was dark and raining—I accelerated as I was leaving Bensheim and suddenly hit something which, in the poor visibility, I initially thought was a big cardboard box. As it turned out, it was a person crossing the street. Worse still, when I looked at the person lying injured on the ground, I recognized his face: It was the partner of my theatre director. He had been responsible for the stage design. He was seriously injured, but fortunately survived. My car was badly damaged and had to be replaced. I visited him in the hospital and expressed how deeply sorry I was. A judge ruled that I was partly to blame for the accident, as I had been driving a bit too fast. In any case, this sad incident led me to give up my budding career as an actor.

But acting was not the only hobby I pursued during our years in Lorsch. At one point, Aline suggested that I buy a model railway for Patrick, believing he would take great joy in it. Initially hesitant, I eventually warmed to the idea—then, quite unexpectedly, found myself completely enthralled by it. What began as a gift for a child soon became a shared project, and then, increasingly, my own quiet passion.

We cleared out one of the cellar rooms and installed a large table board on which to plan a capacious railway landscape. I decided on the Fleischmann N scale—a more compact alternative to the more common Märklin sets—allowing for greater complexity in a relatively confined space. I began sketching an intricate layout, centered around a bustling train station with tracks winding outward in elegant loops, encircling a growing cityscape. The miniature buildings—each to be carefully assembled—formed a tiny world of their own, complete with streets, lampposts, street cars, and trees (Images).

Patrick, of course, was eager to be involved. At first, I allowed him only limited participation, as he was still quite young and the construction required a certain precision. But he delighted in the motion of the trains, and together we would watch as the InterCity Express and other trains wove their way through tunnels and across bridges, faithfully following the paths I had designed for them. For a time, the model train brought joy to both Patrick and me. But, as with so many things, the enchantment did not last forever. Another important professional change was about to take place.

Shortly after my last trip to Pakistan in 1988, a somber shadow fell over the Christian Blind Mission. Siegfried Wiesinger, our director and the formidable architect of CBM's rise, took his own life. The news came like a thunderclap. One night, he directed the exhaust fumes inward into his car and awaited death by carbon monoxide poisoning. It was an act both deliberate and tragic.

Some segments of the German media had circulated unfounded reports alleging the misuse of donations by CBM. The allegations were later proven entirely false, but the damage to Wiesinger's reputation—and perhaps to his sense of personal honor—had been done. For a man who had poured so much of himself into building CBM into one of Germany's most respected development organizations, the public mistrust must have cut with surgical cruelty.

One of the hard-earned lessons I drew from this tragic incident was the crucial importance of cultivating strong relationships with the media—even for a nonprofit organization such as CBM. Such connections serve not only to inform the public but also to guard against the kind of misconceptions and misunderstandings that unfolded in this case. Wiesinger, despite his many talents and creative brilliance, had failed to grasp the quiet power of public relations—a blind spot that ultimately contributed to his own undoing. In neglecting the media, he underestimated its ability not just to shape narratives, but to unravel them.

The news of his suicide reverberated through the halls of CBM like a tolling bell. Shock and disbelief settled over us. I could not help but revisit my last meeting with him. I had been in his office only days before. He had seemed withdrawn, preoccupied, but I had assumed it to be just a passing burden, the sort that came and went with the pressures of leadership. I later asked myself whether I should have stayed longer, asked more probing questions, sought a private conversation. Could a gesture, a word, have altered the course of what he had already decided in his mind? I will never know.

As the chairman of the workers' association, I was given the difficult and delicate task of addressing the assembled CBM staff at the memorial service. It was one of the most sobering speeches I have ever given. I spoke frankly—about his extraordinary accomplishments, his tireless dedication, and yes, about the complexities of his leadership and temperament. Despite the storms, he had built something remarkable out of almost nothing. His legacy, though scarred by an unjust ending, deserves to be remembered in its fullness.

Some time after the funeral, I had an encounter with Wiesinger's widow. In a quiet moment, she handed me his personal notebook—a small worn volume filled with the familiar traces of his unmistakable handwriting. Among its pages, she pointed out the raw and painful testimony of a man driven to his end not by guilt, but by despair. In terse, sometimes barely legible lines, he had outlined the motives behind his final act: the unrelenting storm of media attacks, yes, but more cutting still were his reflections on colleagues and friends—those he had once trusted—who had turned away from him in the hour of greatest need. It seemed that, in the reckoning of his final days, he saw himself abandoned and deserted.

And yet, reading those handwritten lines, I was struck not just by the bitterness, but by a deep, almost tragic clarity. He seemed to have recognized, in part, that he was reaping the consequences of his own temperament—his outbursts, his often volatile leadership style. He was, in many respects, a difficult man. But still, for many of us, his death left a void that could not be filled. He was, after all, the driving force behind CBM's transformation from a modest, near-defunct mission society into one of the most widely supported aid organizations in the country, even in the world. Friends and colleagues, myself among them, often recalled with admiration the scale and vision of what he had built—his boundless energy, his brilliance as a fundraiser, his instinct for purpose.

Wiesinger had also recognized that the organization he had built was entering into a new phase where some things would have to be handled differently going forward. Only a few weeks before his death, he had told us: "I know things will have to be changed in the future, but I cannot be the one to implement those changes." I felt that this was a judicious and self-conscious recognition of his own limitations.

In the wake of his death, the Board moved quickly to appoint a new CEO: the Reverend Christian Garms. In many respects, Garms was a fitting choice—intelligent, articulate, a man of considerable administrative skill. He stepped into the role with poise and a sense of continuity, but it did not take long before other aspects of his leadership began to surface. Unlike Wiesinger's fiery idealism, Garms brought with him a calculating precision, and, as it soon became evident, a keen appetite for personal power.

On multiple occasions, he seemed to maneuver staff members into precarious positions—subtle shifts in responsibility, quiet removals from decision-making circles—all seemingly designed to consolidate and enhance his own influence. He underestimated, however, the collective intelligence and memory of those who had served under Wiesinger's tenure. His subtle strategies and machinations, though cloaked in professionalism, did not go unnoticed. Discontent began to simmer beneath the surface, and eventually, it boiled over. The very traits that had given him ascendancy became the cause of his downfall. In the end, it was not a coup, but a quiet consensus that ended his term.

But before things came to a head with Garms, he approached me, in the Spring of 1988, with a peculiar proposition: Would I be willing to accompany Magdalena Wiesinger on a journey to the **PHILIPPINES**? At that time, Mrs. Wiesinger held the title of President of *CBM International*—the organization's increasingly influential global branch. There was little doubt that the title had been granted to her, at least in part, in recognition of her being the wife of the director, rather than because of her own qualifications. Within the organization, whispers circulated questioning her leadership style, her aloofness, and, not least, her strained relationships with key colleagues. Garms and I both understood that travelling with her came with its risks. Still, I accepted the assignment with a quiet confidence that I could manage the interpersonal challenges she might present.

Our itinerary took us first to Manila for an official meeting with our Filipino partner organizations. The atmosphere was cordial, and the presence of Mrs. Wiesinger lent an air of gravitas to the proceedings. During the conference, we were invited to an official audience with the President of the Philippines, Mrs. Corazón Aquino, who had risen to power following the "People Power Revolution"—a historic, bloodless uprising that had unseated the dictatorial regime of Ferdinand Marcos. Her rise to the presidency marked a turning point for the Philippines; her composure and moral clarity stood in stark contrast to the bombast of her predecessor. We were able to speak to her about the work of CBM and what we were doing for the blind and disabled in the Philippines through our local partners. Aquino was interested and posed a number of questions. Meeting President Aquino was a humbling experience and stayed with me.

After the meeting with our Filipino partners, we visited several CBM-supported projects. On one visit I was taken by helicopter to a school for the hearing-impaired in Paowin (Image: Helicopter). We were impressed by the beauty of the place, the warmth of the people there, and the more than modest circumstances under which they lived. Despite heavy clouds and rain, we flew back to Manila. Shortly after takeoff, we noticed that one of the doors of the helicopter was unlocked. The pilot immediately landed in the middle of nowhere, carefully secured the door, and we could continue our journey.

When Mrs. Wiesinger returned to Germany, I remained behind to pursue additional visits—this time to the southern region of the archipelago. My journey took me to Mindanao, the largest of the southern islands, known for its natural beauty but also for its social unrest. From the city of Zamboanga, I boarded a small single-propeller aircraft, a Piper Cherokee, bound for the island of Jolo—a place that even then held a reputation for volatility. Jolo, largely under the control of Muslim separatists, had witnessed sporadic violence and kidnappings, and CBM's presence there was as much an act of faith as of service.

Upon landing at the modest airstrip, I was met not by local aid workers, but by a small convoy of military humvees. I was not just a visitor but, in their eyes, someone to be protected (Image: Kurt with Soldiers). They escorted me into Jolo City, a town that felt, at first glance, like an echo of an earlier

century. Though bustling with people and activity, the usual cacophony of urban life was eerily absent. Private citizens were prohibited from using motor vehicles; instead, the streets flowed with bicycles and softly squeaking rickshaws. It was as if the city operated under a hush, a low hum of caution and constraint.

After my visit to Jolo I flew back to Zamboanga, where we visited Rio Hondo—a poor village precariously built on stilts above the water, its wooden walkways winding through a maze of modest homes (Image: Rio Hondo).

From there, we continued on to Manila, where I visited several other CBM-supported

projects. One of the most haunting stops was "Smokey Mountain," the infamous dumpsite where thousands of people scavenged through mountains of garbage to survive. The poverty I witnessed there surpassed anything I had seen in Bombay or Calcutta. Amid the smoke and refuse, we soon encountered a five-year-old deaf girl—untouched by any form of education or support. Her silent presence spoke volumes. The need was immediate, undeniable.

I left the Philippines with a heavy heart—deeply moved, but also disheartened by the scale of suffering. As I boarded my flight back to Germany,

The visit to Penang had already planted a seed in me. It wasn't just a beautiful island fringed by turquoise waters and swaying palms—it was also livable in every sense of the word. I could never have imagined relocating Aline to some remote outpost in Africa, where daily essentials were scarce and the climate tested one's spirit. But Penang was different. One could find nearly everything needed for modern family life—international schools, reliable infrastructure, a vibrant expatriate community. Prices were reasonable, and the lush, sun-drenched beaches seemed to promise serenity after long working days.

Back in Lorsch, the news of our possible move had not yet trickled down to Patrick. But one afternoon, as he returned from school and threw down his backpack, he made a declaration that caught both of us by surprise: "School is boring. I want an adventure." Aline, never one to miss an opportunity, replied without missing a beat: "Well then, you're in luck. We're moving to Malaysia." The transformation in him was immediate. What had moments before been dull routine now gave way to curiosity and anticipation. From that day forward, the move became *his* adventure too.

At the CBM office, however, things were not unfolding with quite the same sense of ease. Christian Garms—true to his political style—attempted a maneuver. Although he had initially offered me the position of *Regional Director*, he now claimed I would go as "Assistant to the Regional Director." It was a typical Garms stratagem: a quiet demotion wrapped in bureaucratic wording, a means to consolidate his own position by weakening others. I didn't hesitate. "If that's the case, I'm not going," I told him directly. I could see in his eyes that he hadn't expected this level of defiance. But he backed down. He had little choice. And the title was restored.

Before I was to relocate to Penang and begin my work in earnest, Gerhard Weiland, my immediate superior, insisted I first embark on a field visit to *SUDAN* and *SOMALIA*. He felt I ought to be tested by hardship, reminded of the raw conditions under which so many of our partner projects operated, before settling into the more comfortable life Penang might offer. So, off I went—first to Sudan.

Khartoum, the capital city, was another world entirely. I had seen hardship before, but Khartoum challenged me anew. The air shimmered with heat—dry, oppressive, almost sterile in its aridity. Temperatures hovered between 45 and 50 degrees Celsius (110 to 120 Fahrenheit), the sun beating down like a punishment. Transport was unreliable; buses were packed to bursting or entirely absent, taxis rare and erratic. Simply navigating the city was a feat of endurance.

And yet, amid that harshness, I met a remarkable man—a Sudanese doctor who had established an educational and rehabilitative project for the disabled. He had studied partially in Europe and had absorbed both its intellectual rigor and its humanitarian values. Rarely had I encountered a man of such quiet depth, unwavering ethics, and clarity of thought. He had even translated *The Little Prince* into Sudanese Arabic, a gesture that revealed both his poetic sensibility and his pedagogical instinct. He was also deeply critical of his military government, unafraid to voice his concerns even in uncertain company. As I listened to this African speak, eloquent and resolute, I admired his courage—but I also feared for him. Men like him were rarely left undisturbed for long in such regimes.

From Khartoum, I had been instructed to continue my journey northward to visit CBM-supported initiatives beyond the capital. My destination was Atbara, an arid, sun-bleached city on the edge of the desert. I boarded a domestic flight in the afternoon, seated next to a young Sudanese man *en route* to Egypt. He, like myself, would have to spend the night in Atbara before continuing his journey.

When we disembarked around five o'clock, the air hit us like an oven door flung open. The thermometer still hovered at a staggering 46 degrees Celsius. My fellow traveler, evidently well acquainted with local conditions, recommended a modest guesthouse where we could rest. That evening, we slept outdoors, beneath the stars, stretched out on woven mats in the relative coolness of the desert night. By midnight, the heat had relented, and the temperature had fallen to a pleasant 20 degrees Celsius. The stars above Atbara, unpolluted by city lights, felt infinite and strangely comforting.

The following day I visited the director of a school for the blind, along with several other individuals involved in our programs there. They received me with warmth and dignity, despite the obvious strain of working under such difficult conditions. In the course of our conversation, the school director inquired where I had stayed during my time in Khartoum. I named the hotel—well known, it turned out, for being one of the city's finest. A single night's stay there cost about 100 U.S. dollars. He nodded slowly, then remarked that his monthly salary amounted to almost exactly the same sum. For a moment, we sat in mutual silence, the uncomfortable weight of inequality hanging between us. There was no need for commentary. The numbers said enough.

Later that day, I met a young Sudanese woman involved in rehabilitative work, a bright and committed individual whose presence suggested resilience born of adversity. She turned to me during our discussion and asked, almost in a whisper: *"Why do we have to suffer so much here?"* Her voice carried no anger, only weariness. Was it the poverty, the heat, the stifling burden of survival in such a place? I wanted to offer something—some theological, sociological, or humanitarian rationale—but I had none. Her question fell into the silence like a stone into deep water. I was at a loss.

My return to Khartoum was marred by delay. The flight from Atbara was postponed just long enough for me to miss my onward connection to Nairobi. I watched the aircraft, its engines idling on the runway, knowing full well it was my flight—yet powerless to board it. A Kafkaesque dance with logistics followed as I sought out a travel agent in the stifling capital.

Khartoum, as ever, was unreliable in its infrastructure. Daily blackouts were the norm. Some offices were equipped with generators to power fans or air conditioners, but many—like the small travel agency I found—were not. Stepping inside, I was immediately struck by the suffocating heat. It must have been at least 55, perhaps even 60 degrees Celsius. The air stood still, thick and dry like the inside of a kiln. My skin prickled, and my clothes clung to me like a second, unwelcome skin. I staggered outside again, gasping. *I cannot go back in there,* I told myself. But I had no choice. The flight had to be rebooked.

So I returned, pushing my way through the heat, sweat pouring down my back and forehead. When I finally emerged again, ticket in hand, I was drenched. The air outside, though still hot, now felt merciful by comparison.

The next day, I flew onward to Nairobi, and from there to Mogadishu, the sprawling and sun-baked capital of Somalia. I had come to visit an eye-medical program supported by CBM, and to better understand the conditions under which our local partners were working.

Whereas Sudan's inferno had been marked by a dry and searing heat, Somalia presented an altogether different kind of challenge. The air was thick with moisture, saturated to near-complete humidity. At a mere 32 degrees Celsius—hardly extreme by African standards—it was not the temperature itself that overwhelmed, but the stifling, inescapable dampness that clung to the skin and weighed down every breath. One could not escape it, indoors or out.

Yet despite the physical discomfort, I managed to keep my bearings. I asked questions, listened attentively, and tried to grasp the full scope of the challenges faced by those delivering medical care in one of the most fragile and underdeveloped nations in the world. Their work—difficult, heroic, and often thankless—took place in an environment that demanded both grit and grace.

By the time I returned to Germany, I carried with me a quiet, almost defiant conviction: that nothing could shake me anymore. I had seen places where survival itself was a daily achievement, where heat, hardship, and instability pressed down with equal force. And yet, in those very places, I had met men and women who still believed in the power of service and the dignity of care. If they could carry on, then surely, so could I.

Penang and East Asia

Aline, Patrick, and I began preparations for our move to Asia with a mixture of anticipation and apprehension. We packed up our lives in Lorsch, stored all our belongings in a warehouse, and boarded a plane bound for Bangkok, and from there, onward to Penang. Our arrival in Penang was met with gracious hospitality: My colleague Bill Brohier received us at the airport and welcomed us into his home, offering a soft landing in what was to become our new life.

But Penang greeted us not only with warmth in the human sense—it did so quite literally. The humidity was staggering, hovering near saturation at all times – as I had experienced it in Somalia. Rain fell nearly every day, drenching the lush tropical landscape, while temperatures remained stubbornly in the low thirties Celsius. Still fatigued from the journey, Aline and Patrick were visibly dismayed. The air was thick, and their spirits quickly sank. "We can't live here," they murmured. "We'll go back to Germany." It was, unmistakably, a moment of culture shock.

Yet I had seen this before, and I knew better than to panic. The initial discomfort would pass. Penang had its own way of weaving itself into one's affections. And so it did.

Before long, we found a spacious and comfortable house to call home (Image: Penang House). It allowed us room to breathe, to settle in, and to begin our new routine. Still, the climate left its mark. I recall one particular day when a plumber came to fix our malfunctioning water heater. He arrived fully dressed, methodically going about his work, while I—barefoot, in nothing more than shorts and a thin T-shirt—stood by in the sweltering

heat. And yet it was I who was dripping with sweat, while he worked with stoic composure. It was a lesson in adaptation: the body, like the mind, needs time to learn the rhythm of a new climate. As I would come to learn, about six months.

And then, gradually and almost unnoticed, the unbearable became comfortable—even pleasurable. Penang revealed itself in layers. George Town, with its rich colonial architecture and vibrant cultural tapestry, offered everything one could possibly need—and much more—at prices that made European shopping seem extravagant (Image: Penang Shopping). Evenings were often spent by the sea, strolling near the grand hotels, where the breeze off the water would bring a brief but welcome reprieve.

As for meals, we embraced the local way. Hawker stalls became our go-to: simple roadside eateries where flavors danced in unpretentious dishes, and where one could dine like royalty for a modest sum. It was there, among the aromas of garlic, ginger, and lemongrass, that we began to feel at home.

One of our first important decisions in Penang was choosing a school for Patrick. The options were clear: a well-regarded British institution or an evangelical American school. I had long thought it valuable for Patrick to gain a sense of the "American way of life," and so I gently urged him toward the latter. He enrolled in the American school, albeit with some initial hesitation. I also managed to persuade the school's director to place him in a higher grade than his age would normally have allowed—convinced, as I was, of his readiness. Time would prove the decision sound: Patrick would complete his secondary school at the age of barely eighteen.

The beginning, however, was not without challenges. Patrick was not yet fluent in English, and those first few weeks were marked by unease. We could sense his discomfort—his sense of being an outsider in an unfamiliar linguistic and cultural world. But children are resilient in ways adults often forget. After a month or so, he began to find his footing. He understood more, spoke more, and slowly blended into his new environment. His English improved with astonishing speed, and to this day, he still speaks with the unmistakable trace of an American accent.

While Patrick attended school, Aline took on the considerable task of managing our new household. She sought contact with other European expatriates, hoping to build the kind of informal network that becomes vital when one is living far from home. Our house, though spacious and comfortable, came with some unexpected visitors. There were snakes—one of which turned out to be a rattlesnake—and, in one memorable instance, a large monitor lizard more than a meter and a half long wandered in, utterly unfazed by Aline's attempts to shoo it away. It lingered, inspecting its surroundings with imperial indifference, and was only coaxed out again after considerable effort. Yet aside from these rare intrusions, Aline grew to appreciate Penang deeply. The beaches, golden and lush, were a balm to the senses, and she often spent her afternoons there.

Penang was also home to some traditional Hindu festivals, the most prominent being the Thaipusam event which is dedicated to Lord Murugan, the god of war. Thaipusam is an occasion for devotion and religious commitment unlike any other. Many devotees, called *kavadis,* practice flesh mortification by inserting spikes through their cheeks, their tongues or their backs (Images: Indian Kavadis). Another important Penang festival was Deepavali, the festival of lights. It is a rather joyful time, similar to Christmas for Christians.

Patrick, too, grew to love the rhythms of Penang. He got his first bicycle, his first video camera, and began training in Taekwondo—eventually earning his second black belt, a quiet testament to his growing discipline and strength. His spirit of adventure soon led us deeper into Malaysia's untouched heart: the *Taman Negara*—a primeval rainforest, among the oldest on Earth, spanning over 4,000 square kilometers of untamed wilderness (Images: Kurt and Patrick in Taman Negara).

There, Patrick and I spent several unforgettable days immersed in nature's embrace. We hiked beneath towering canopies, guided by the calls of monkeys and hidden creatures. We swam in the cool, flowing waters of the

Tahan River; and at night, sheltered in a humble tent we had carried with us, we drifted to sleep beneath a tapestry of stars and forest murmurs. It was, in every sense, a journey of discovery—of nature, of self, and of the bond between father and son. An experience that lingers not only in memory, but in spirit.

As for my profession, I was soon immersed in my new duties—either at the CBM office in Penang or traveling across the region, visiting our supported projects. The work was intense, but also immensely rewarding, offering a profound window into both human need and human resilience across Southeast Asia.

Since the CBM Regional Office in Bangkok was unoccupied at the time, I had been asked to temporarily step in and oversee its responsibilities. The Bangkok office had a wide and diverse mandate: it supervised projects in no fewer than eight countries—Cambodia, China, Korea, Laos, Myanmar (formerly Burma), Thailand, Vietnam, and the most recent addition, Mongolia.

Meanwhile, the Penang office under the leadership of my colleague Bill Brohier focused on Indonesia, the Philippines, Papua New Guinea, and a scattering of Pacific Island nations. Between the two regions, my travel schedule became extraordinarily full. In 1991 alone, I was away from Penang on official duty for precisely 181 days—exactly half the year. When in Penang, I still had to take care of correspondence and other urgent matters at the office, but the evenings were spent with the family.

In November 1990, I undertook my first journey to **CHINA**. The occasion was a high-level conference on rehabilitation, held in Beijing and organized by Deng Pufang, the eldest son of Deng Xiaoping—the architect of China's transformation into a socialist market economy. Deng Pufang himself bore the scars of China's turbulent political past. During the Cultural Revolution, he had been assaulted by the Red Guards and sustained spinal injuries that left him paraplegic. He went on to become a prominent advocate for the disabled in China, founding the *China Welfare Fund for the Disabled* and using his influence to push for structural reforms in the areas of accessibility, education, and rehabilitation.

The conference was held in the imposing *Great Hall of the People*, which flanks the western edge of the vast Tiananmen Square. Best known as the meeting site of the National People's Congress, the Hall is an architectural colossus capable of accommodating up to 10,000 people. While plenary sessions took place in the grand auditorium, a number of smaller, more specialized meetings were held in adjoining conference rooms. The atmosphere was formal, but not unwelcoming, and I found the exchanges both informative and thought-provoking.

During a brief interlude between sessions, I managed to visit the nearby Forbidden City, just north of the square. Wandering through the ancient halls and courtyards that had once been the home of 24 emperors from the Ming and Qing dynasties, I was struck by the grandeur and symbolism of the place. It was a reminder that China, for all its rapid modernization, carried within it a deep and intricate historical memory—one that often revealed itself in subtle ways during my later interactions with Chinese partners.

Following my first visit to Beijing, I boarded a domestic flight to Nanjing, the ancient capital of several Chinese dynasties and, at the time, the headquarters of the *Amity Foundation*—our principal partner organization in China. Amity, a faith-based NGO with strong roots in the Chinese Protestant community, had taken on the role of coordinating rehabilitation and medical projects across various provinces. During my visit, they convened a conference for Chinese partners, which gave me the opportunity to meet numerous representatives from projects CBM had just begun to support. It was my first exposure to the breadth and complexity of implementing disability-related initiatives in a country where the scale of both need and bureaucracy was enormous. The atmosphere was cautiously optimistic; I sensed in our Chinese colleagues both curiosity and a willingness to collaborate across cultural and ideological boundaries.

Before the year drew to a close, my itinerary took me to **VIETNAM** and **CAMBODIA**. Southern Vietnam, with its lush rice paddies and ever-present aroma of street food, offered not only a warm welcome but also introduced me to a range of dedicated people who were implementing projects with both competence and heart. I was deeply moved by their hospitality, often extended with modest means but sincere warmth.

During this visit, I also had the opportunity to explore the infamous Cu Chi tunnels near Ho Chi Minh City. These subterranean passages—spanning over 200 kilometers—had been carved out by Viet Cong soldiers as a vast, interconnected network of hiding places, supply routes, field hospitals, and storage depots during the long and brutal conflict with South Vietnam and the United States. Navigating the narrow tunnels, I couldn't help but admire the ingenuity and resilience of the people who had lived and fought in such confined and perilous conditions. The contrast between their small, nimble frames and the larger stature of the American soldiers—who could only advance through the tunnels on their knees—highlighted the tactical advantage the Viet Cong had created for themselves.

The Americans, frustrated by the elusive enemy beneath the earth, responded with overwhelming force—dropping thousands of tons of bombs on the surrounding jungle in an effort to obliterate the tunnel systems. Much of the landscape was reduced to a cratered wasteland, a moonscape scarred by the violence of war. Standing in that terrain, I felt not only the weight of history but also a deepened sense of purpose in our work: to support healing and rebuilding where destruction had once ruled.

I knew of no country in Southeast Asia where the daily struggle for survival was as visible and all-consuming as in Vietnam. The monthly salaries even of educated people was minimal. Medical doctors told me their salary was no more than 10 dollars a month, barely enough to purchase food. The nation, ravaged by decades of war and economic isolation, was in dire straits. The government teetered on the edge of insolvency, its resources stretched thin, and its health infrastructure in tatters. Amidst these conditions, CBM focused its efforts on eye medical services, an area of urgent need and promising impact.

At that time, it was estimated that Vietnam had more than half a million blind individuals. Of these, at least 300,000 could potentially regain their sight through a simple cataract operation. Yet the country managed to perform only about 12,000 such surgeries each year—a mere drop in the ocean of need. The reasons for this tragic gap were manifold: a widespread lack of public awareness, a severe shortage of surgical instruments and medications, and perhaps most devastatingly, the absence of reliable transport to help patients reach one of the few hospitals equipped to carry out the procedures. The backlog was not just a statistic—it represented hundreds of thousands of lives diminished by preventable blindness.

Following this sobering visit, I flew to Phnom Penh, Cambodia's war-battered capital. There, the atmosphere was a curious blend of trauma and tentative hope. The country had only recently emerged from one of the darkest chapters of modern history—the near-genocide under the Khmer Rouge, followed by years of civil war. But now, with the signing of a fragile peace agreement by all warring factions and the prospect of general elections on the horizon, there was a collective sense that healing might finally begin.

CBM was just beginning its involvement in Cambodia at that time. Toward the end of the year, an ophthalmologist couple had taken up residence to initiate an eye care program. Their presence felt like the first stirrings of rain on parched land. The need was staggering: Four ophthalmologists served the entire population of eight million, and all were concentrated in Phnom Penh. Beyond the capital, there was almost nothing—no eye services, no outreach, no surgical capacity.

The broader disability landscape was equally dire. There were an estimated 30,000 amputees, most of them casualties of the countless landmines still strewn across the countryside. In addition, around 8,000 people were blind, with little to no support available. The civil war had not only destroyed infrastructure but also the social fabric necessary for compassionate care. In such a setting, CBM's presence could be more than just helpful—it could be transformative.

As the year drew to a close, Aline and I wondered how we would spend Christmas. We didn't have a Christmas tree, nor could we expect any snow. There were a few Christmas lights around Penang, but overall, the festive spirit was lacking. To make up for it a little, we took the cable car up to Penang Hill on Christmas Eve, in order to enjoy a beautiful view of the city lights of George Town. It was our *ersatz* for a "christmas tree." I then read a Christmas story I had brought with me, we lit sparklers, and then indulged in homemade Christmas cookies. That was our Christmas Eve experience in Penang. We did so again the following years.

In early 1991, I had the opportunity to visit a number of CBM-supported projects in Thailand, each visit adding another layer of insight into the region's multifaceted challenges. Soon after, I found myself back in Penang, tasked with organizing a CBM Co-Workers Meeting. This event, held in a Penang hotel, brought together CBM staff from across the region: eye doctors, teachers for the blind and those for the deaf, and other specialists. The goal was to disseminate important information regarding CBM's regulations, and for all co-workers to report on their ongoing projects. All participants were eager to share their experiences and challenges, and were united in their commitment to a shared mission.

By March 1991, I traveled to Bensheim, Germany, for one of the regular director's meetings, which were critical for aligning strategies and discussing future initiatives. In any given year, I had to attend two such meetings: one in the spring, when the trees began to blossom, the other in the fall, when leaves turned yellow and red. These visits to Germany gave me a welcome reprieve from the Asian heat and humidity. Through these Executives' Meetings, the global nature of CBM's work was becoming more evident to me—projects in different corners of the world, all interconnected through a common vision of service to the disabled.

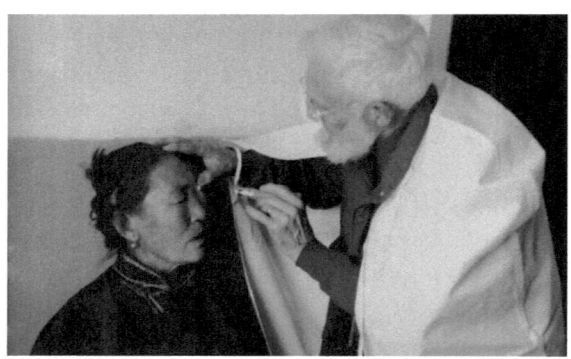

Later that spring, I embarked on a journey that took me back to Thailand, where I visited additional projects, and on to *CHINA* and *TIBET*. This trip also led to a collaboration with Dr. Norval Christy, the trusted colleague and expert from Taxila Eye Hospital (Image: Dr. Christy).

That journey took us first to Anhui Province, not far from Nanjing, before heading to the more remote Qinghai Province, in whose capital Xining we visited their eye hospital. From there, we ventured to Lhasa in Tibet.

In Tibet, we were accompanied at all times by a government official, assigned to "look after us" and ensure that everything proceeded according to plan. Amid such constraints, our mission remained clear: to assess local hospitals and explore ways to support them in strengthening their eye care services. One key initiative was arranging training for Tibetan doctors in cataract surgery—a crucial step toward alleviating the widespread blindness afflicting the region.

On evening walks through the city of Lhasa, we saw Tibetan women in quiet devotion, prostrating themselves along the streets—embodying a spiritual dedication that permeated everyday life. In Tibetan Buddhism, full-body prostration is a gesture of deep humility and respect for the Buddha and his teachings. I found this practice rather ghastly and humiliating.

We also visited one of the monasteries, where the stillness of the monks stood in poignant contrast to the suffering we had witnessed in the clinics—a serene counterpoint to the human struggles unfolding beyond the monastery walls.

One of the places I had hoped to see was the iconic Potala Palace, perched atop the Red Hill. But I made the decision not to hike up the hill to visit it. The high altitude of Lhasa—at 3,500 meters—was a constant challenge for me, and while I managed relatively well during the daytime, the nights were outright agonizing. I developed a severe headache due to the thin air, and sleep was nearly impossible. To assist my breathing, I was provided with a sheepskin bag filled with oxygen, which became my only solace during those painful nights. And as for the Potama Palace, I could only take a photograph from a distance (Image: Potama Palace).

I decided to shorten our stay in Lhasa to just three days, recognizing that the altitude was taking a toll on my body, and there was much more to see in China.

We flew onward to Chengdu, the capital of Sichuan Province, where we met with the eye doctors at the university hospital. They were eager to share their work and offered us an in-depth look at the healthcare systems in place.

They also arranged for us to visit a district hospital and a small rural clinic, providing us with a broader understanding of the challenges they faced in extending eyemedical services to remote areas.

One of the most memorable experiences during this visit was the time we spent in a small village, which had its own modest health station. It was a far cry from the larger, more well-equipped hospitals we had seen, but the villagers' commitment to helping each other was evident. That evening, the village elders invited us to dinner, a gesture of kindness that was typical for Chinese hospitality. They gifted me a set of lacquerware items, which, though simple in comparison to other rarities I had purchased in China, still holds a special significance for me. I have kept those pieces to this day as a token of the humble generosity with which the people of that village shared their culture and lives with us.

But I received yet another, most curious gift: a pig's head. It was offered to us as an additional souvenir, and while it struck me as somewhat awkward, I graciously accepted it, thanking the donors profusely for their kind gesture. But once we boarded the bus to begin our return journey, I found myself in a bit of a dilemma. I wasn't quite sure what to do with this special gift, and in a moment of deliberate forgetfulness, I left the pig's head behind in the bus as we disembarked.

Aside from the peculiar souvenirs, another striking aspect of this trip was the landscape of Sichuan. The steep mountain slopes were unlike anything I had seen before. The locals had ingeniously converted these steep hill-sides into terraced fields, planting and harvesting crops in what seemed like impossible conditions. The sheer determination and adaptability required to cultivate food in such rugged terrain was impressive. I couldn't help but marvel at how these people had made the most of every inch of land available to them, turning even the most challenging landscapes into sources of sustenance.

May 1991 marked the beginning of a new chapter, as I undertook my first official journey on behalf of the *Penang Regional Office*. The trip took me far into the South Pacific, with stops in the island nations of *FIJI* and *VANUATU*. In Suva, the capital of Fiji, I attended the inaugural meeting of the *Pacific Islands Council*, a promising initiative dedicated to improving the education and rehabilitation of blind and disabled people across the scattered Pacific islands. The meeting brought together various stakeholders of the region, and despite the geographic isolation of many of the islands, there was a clear sense of solidarity and shared purpose among the participants.

On my way back, I made a stopover in Vanuatu, an archipelago that was still in the early stages of developing services for the disabled. I was eager to learn what steps were being taken, also in terms of eyemedical care. While the infrastructure was modest, there was an unmistakable will to improve conditions, and CBM's presence was beginning to make a difference.

The following month, in June, I made my first journey to *NORTH VIET-NAM*. This trip held special importance, as it was a chance to witness first-hand the progress made thanks to the collaborative efforts between CBM and the Institute of Ophthalmology in Hanoi. On this trip, I visited the cities of Hai Phong (Images: Hai Phong) and Hue, following up on earlier visits

by Dr. Norval Christy. We were able to provide essential eye equipment and medicines, and support was extended for further training — doctors were sent to India, where they could develop their skills, and groups of educators and government officials traveled to Thailand to explore best practices in inclusive education.

I also had the opportunity to meet with Vietnam's Minister of Health, a gentle, soft-spoken man whose kindness was palpable (Image: Kurt and the Minister of Health). Despite the overwhelming challenges his ministry faced, he received us with humility and gratitude. CBM had already provided essential equipment and ophthalmic medicines valued at around half a million dollars—no small contribution in a country where even basic medical supplies were scarce.

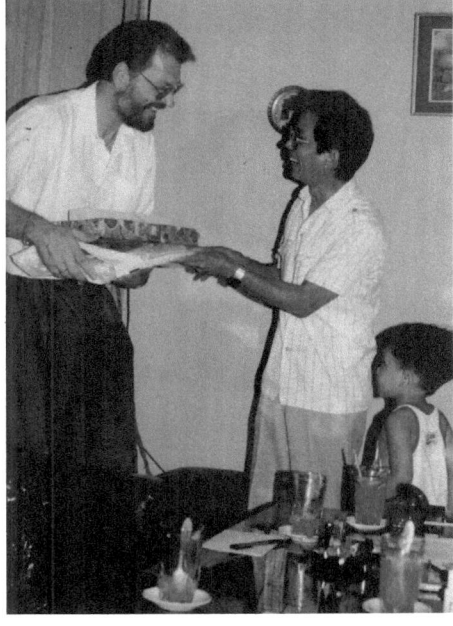

By August, I found myself once again in Thailand, making the rounds of various CBM-supported projects. Then came September and with it, my return to Bensheim for the annual budget deliberations and Executives'

Meeting. Balancing field realities with administrative responsibilities was never easy, yet it was this very contrast that kept my perspective grounded.

Back in Penang, I barely had time to settle before my next journey called — this time to **CHINA** and **MONGOLIA**. In October 1991, I first travelled to Bangkok and on to Kunming, the capital of Yunnan Province in China's southwest, before flying on to Beijing and Ulan Bator.

Kunming was a city of moderate climate and striking natural beauty, but what brought me there was the large provincial institute for the Deaf and Blind. This was a major hub for special education in the region, serving 77 blind pupils and over 300 deaf students. I was encouraged to see that early steps were being taken to teach deaf students to speak, not just to sign — a notable shift in pedagogical approach. It was clear that this institute played a central role in shaping the lives of children with disabilities across Yunnan, and we were eager to support and strengthen its efforts.

While in Kunming, I also visited the famous Stone Forest — a surreal landscape of towering limestone formations that resembled petrified trees. The jagged rocks, stretching into the sky like frozen sentinels, created an atmosphere of mystery and quiet grandeur. It was like nothing else I had ever seen — a truly unique natural wonder that left a lasting impression (Images).

From Kunming, I flew north to Beijing to meet Dr. Norval Christy again, recently retired from the Taxila Eye Hospital in Pakistan. His experience and insight into eye care systems made him an invaluable travel partner. For the evening dinner we had at the hotel together, I ordered a dish of fried scorpions which I found absolutely delicious. The next day, we flew to Ulan Bator, the capital of Mongolia.

In the aftermath of the Soviet Union's collapse, this country was plunged into a period of deep uncertainty. Communism had all but vanished, yet a functioning market economy had not yet emerged to take its place. There were shortages of nearly everything—goods that once arrived from Russia and other Eastern Bloc na-

tions had simply stopped coming. Unemployment soared, poverty deepened, and decades of centralized planning had smothered any sense of entrepreneurial initiative. Banknotes had become little more than pick-up vouchers, useful only if goods happened to be available. The Mongolian currency, in practical terms, was nearly worthless.

Yet amid the hardship, there were also positive signs of resilience. The communists had left behind a few functional legacies—chief among them, a centralized underground heating system in Ulan Bator that kept homes and buildings warm during the bitter winter months. They had also established a surprisingly far-reaching infrastructure of medical services, extending deep into the countryside. There was a solid number of general practitioners and ophthalmologists still at work.

We visited the eye department of the central university hospital in the capital, then flew to a medical center in Arkhanggai, about 500 kilometers west, and further still to a small rural clinic. The flights, aboard aging Mongolian aircrafts, were adventures in themselves. While Mongolia's medical infrastructure remained intact, the real issue was the lack of essential supplies—medicines, needles, instruments. In discussions with one of the country's first eye doctors, we compiled a list of urgently needed items: slit lamps, ophthalmoscopes, cataract kits, and basic eye medications.

In rural Mongolia, we caught a glimpse of everyday life (Image). Most memorable were the traditional round homes—called *ger* in Mongolian, *yurt* in English. Built on a wooden frame and wrapped in thick layers of sheep's wool, the *ger* is both sturdy and surprisingly cozy (Images). Inside, a *ger* is colorful and welcoming, with a single large space that serves as bedroom, living room and kitchen for up to fifteen people.

Many Mongolians are semi-nomadic; when the time comes to move, the *ger* is dismantled and packed within an hour, then transported to a new location dictated by pasture, wind, and water availability. Despite temperature extremes—from +40°C in summer to -40°C in winter (+100 to -40 Fahrenheit)—the *ger* offers remarkable insulation, keeping families cool in the heat and warm in the cold. It is an elegant solution to an unforgiving climate and landscape. To keep me warm, I was given a typical Mongolian "deel," a large overcoat that protected me from the unfriendly coldness (Image: Kurt dressed in deel on a Mongolian horse).

Back in Ulan Bator, we visited the Special School for the Blind and Deaf, where around 500 hearing-impaired and 100 visually impaired children were enrolled. The school provided food and lodging free of charge, yet it could not accommodate all children in need. Services for the blind and deaf were still very rudimentary, and the idea of integrated education had yet to take root.

From Ulan Bator, we flew back to Beijing and continued on to Nanjing to visit the Amity Foundation. We reviewed current initiatives and explored ways to improve and expand them, including strategies for training new eye doctors. As my visit drew to a close, I said farewell to the Amity staff and to Dr. Christy, who returned to the United States, while I made my way back to Penang via Guangzhou and Singapore.

My next journey took me to **SOUTH KOREA**—a country that, in many ways, surprised me more than any other. I hadn't anticipated the sheer level of modern development I would encounter. South Korea stood shoulder to shoulder with industrial powerhouses like Germany, Japan, and the United States in terms of modernization and standard of living. Its rapid transformation from post-war devastation to economic success was nothing short of remarkable.

Seoul, the capital city, left a vivid impression, not only for its scale and energy but also for its deeply rooted Christian faith. Countless churches adorned the skyline, each marked by illuminated crosses glowing above the rooftops—symbols of a spiritual revival that had taken hold after the Korean Civil War. Perhaps most striking of all was the *Full Gospel Church*, boasting a congregation of 100,000 worshippers, making it one of the largest in the world.

When it came to education for the blind, however, South Korea still lagged behind in one important area: the concept of *integration*—what we now refer to as *inclusion*—had yet to take hold. Segregation was still the norm, not only in schools but even in church communities. Blind worshippers often gathered in their own churches which were equipped with barrier-free facilities which were lacking in most mainstream churches.

During my stay, I visited a rehabilitation center for blind adults, many of whom had lost their sight due to glaucoma. Here, they were taught essential life skills: braille, typing, as well as orientation and mobility (O&M). In the same building complex, the United World Mission (UWM) operated a braille press. Ten skilled braillists transcribed a wide range of materials into braille upon request—offering a crucial service for the blind community.

Before returning to Penang, I made another stop in Bangkok to visit a Cataract Intervention Program, led by two capable and dedicated eye specialists. At the same hospital, I also met Bangkok's Number One ENT specialist, Dr. Soontorn, who impressed me with his fluency in English. I immediately saw potential in him as a valuable regional advisor.

While in Thailand, I also visited a community-based rehabilitation program for persons with disabilities run by the "Daughters of Charity." Time and again, I have come to admire the tireless devotion and professionalism of Catholic Sisters. I joined some of their field workers on home visits to clients in nearby villages and met with seven of the team members, whose grassroots commitment left a deep impression on me.

To round off the trip, I visited a CBM-supported School for the Deaf in Bangkok, being shown around by its director, Dr. Maliwan. She stood out for her sharp competence and excellent command of English, and I left with confidence in the school's leadership and direction.

In January 1992, I embarked on my first official visit to **INDONESIA** on behalf of the Penang office. Though the country comprises more than 14,000 islands, this journey would take me to just two of its biggest: Sumatra and Java. At the time, Indonesia's population stood at nearly 200 million, making it one of the most populous nations on earth.

For this particular trip, I invited Patrick to join me—offering him the chance to experience a new country and culture. One of our first destinations was Balige Hospital in North Sumatra, nestled close to the stunning Lake Toba, a vast crater lake with a sizeable island at its center. Balige town itself was poor, dirty, and lacking in modern infrastructure, yet the hospital was an oasis of calm and spiritual renewal. CBM had previously sponsored the training of one of its eye doctors in India, and by the time of our visit, the hospital was hosting regular weekly eye clinics.

Not far from Balige, in Lagfrom Laguboti, we visited a Center for the Disabled, which also included a community-based outreach program with 23 active field workers. There we met CBM co-worker Liz Cross, who had been seconded to Balige to support the project. Our journey continued northward to the Medan School for the Blind—a facility not yet supported by CBM at the time, but worth observing for future consideration.

From Medan, we flew to Jakarta, Indonesia's bustling capital. One of the highlights there was a visit to a school for multi-handicapped blind children. This once underperforming institution had been transformed into a model center through the dedicated work of CBM co-worker Nicola Crews. Nicola had also authored a manual for teaching multi-handicapped children in the Indonesian language, and her efforts were widely recognized and deeply appreciated. In the city of Bandung, we visited a small braille press, followed by a stop in Cisarua at an agricultural rehabilitation center for blind individuals from rural areas.

Amidst our professional visits, Patrick and I also found time to explore some places of interest. One was the Borobudur Temple in central Java, which dates back to the 9th century (Image: Patrick at Borobudur). This unique temple structure consists of nine stacked platforms (six square and three circular), topped by a central dome. It is decorated with thousands of relief panels and some 500 Buddha statues.

We also visited the Prambanan Temples about 10 miles east of Yogyakarta, which is one of the largest Hindu temple sites in Southeast Asia, second only to Angkor Wat in Cambodia. It, too, was built in the 9th century. It is characterized by its tall und pointed structures, representing the grandeur of ancient Hindu art and architecture: a masterpiece of Indonesia's classical period (Image: Kurt at Prambanan Temples).

In Yogyakarta, we had an unusual encounter: A man approached us, trying to sell us a sloth. The animal's calm, almost meditative slow-motion movements captivated Patrick, who pleaded with me to purchase it. I might have agreed—if I hadn't had good reason to believe that Malaysian customs would never let us bring such a creature across their border.

Patrick and I also got a glimpse of wildlife, visiting a safari park that allowed lions, giraffes, elephants, and other animals to roam freely within large enclosures, giving visitors the sense of encountering them in their natural habitat. Finally, we visited *Taman Mini Indonesia Indah,* a recreational area in Jakarta which displayed many aspects of Indonesian life and culture. One highlight was the *Children's Castle* (Image), another was a small lake on which the main Indonesian islands were displayed in miniature size.

As was tradition during my travels, I sought souvenirs to bring home. For Aline, I usually picked up small but elegant items—silver jars or, on rare occasions, a precious vase. Patrick had a fondness for traditional hand weapons, and we managed to purchase a small ceremonial spear in Indonesia. However, our success was short-lived. When boarding our flight back to Malaysia, airline staff confiscated the spear, promising it would be returned to us upon arrival in Penang.

But when we landed and inquired about the spear, we were told that it had been handed over to the Malaysian customs. The customs officers, however, refused to release it without an official weapons license. Given that such licenses are usually reserved for firearms, we suspected their reluctance was a subtle invitation for a bribe. Not willing to play along, Patrick instead endured a long bureaucratic ordeal to obtain the proper documentation. After finally securing a weapons license, he presented it to customs—and was at last able to take his prized spear home.

In January 1992, I made my first official visit to **BURMA**—known today as Myanmar—in my capacity as Regional Director. I was accompanied by Aline as well as Bob Jaeckle, a seasoned rehabilitation expert.

Burma, I soon discovered, was a country full of contradictions and peculiarities. Upon arrival in Yangon (formerly Rangoon), I had to adjust my watch not by a full hour, as is customary when crossing time zones, but by half an hour—a small but telling oddity.

On the roads, drivers kept to the right-hand side, much like in continental Europe. Yet most vehicles had their steering wheels on the right as well—mirroring British car design—making overtaking a very dangerous gamble. (The former British colony switched to continental driving habits in the seventies, but most cars still dated back to the British era.)

The oddities did not stop there. While Europe was busy dismantling borders and embracing open movement across sovereign countries, Myanmar seemed to move in the opposite direction. Military checkpoints appeared every few kilometers along the main roads, stark reminders of the ever-watchful authoritarian state. Even the currency bore the mark of eccentric governance. Paying for a taxi ride required bills of 45, 90, or 200 kyats—arbitrary denominations that defied logic and made everyday transactions needlessly complicated.

These quirks were symptomatic of a broader dysfunction. The ruling regime styled its system as "The Burmese Way to Socialism," a term that even committed socialists rejected as a distortion of their principles. When that label drew wide criticism, the leadership rebranded the system as "The Burmese Way to Capitalism"—another hollow claim, as no genuine market reforms had taken root. Among the general population, a more cynical and accurate nickname had taken hold: "The Burmese Way to Nowhere."

The government clung to power through a mix of repression and ineffectiveness. Aung San Suu Kyi, who had led her party to a landslide electoral victory, was ousted and placed under house arrest. Democracy had been stifled, and the country remained mired in political paralysis.

Amidst this challenging backdrop, we visited the Education Center for the Blind, an inspiring institution led by U Thein Lwin, a remarkable individual—blind and physically disabled himself—whose energy and creativity had driven the center's growth. Compared to my earlier visit in 1984, the progress was unmistakable. Yet, there was still a clear need for further training, professional development, and specialized seminars (Image).

We also paid visits to several government officials, including the Director General of the Ministry of Social Welfare. Despite some reservations, we agreed to strengthen our collaboration with the Burmese government, hoping that closer cooperation would enhance the reach and impact of rehabilitation and prevention services.

Our itinerary also included a visit to a school for the deaf, a weaving project supporting vocational skills, and a meeting with the Director General of the Ministry of Health. He was genuinely receptive to CBM's interest in contributing to the country's blindness prevention initiatives. At the time, Myanmar faced a staggering backlog of approximately 300,000 cataract cases—many already resulting in complete blindness. CBM committed to supporting cataract surgeries, as well as the local production of spectacles and eye-drops, addressing both immediate needs and long-term sustainability.

While in Burma, we took a private side trip to the ancient city of Bagan in central Myanmar—a place of breathtaking historical and spiritual significance. During the Middle Ages, Bagan had flourished as the capital of the Bagan Empire, becoming its political, economic, and cultural heart. Religion was the dominant force shaping its society; and the city's devotion is still visible today in the grandeur and sheer number of religious structures. The empire's reign came to an end following a Mongolian invasion in the 13th century, but its legacy endures through the exquisite stupas and temples that remain—silent witnesses to the artistic and spiritual dedication of a bygone era.

Bagan is renowned for its numerous Buddhist temples, pagodas, and monasteries (Images next page: Bagan) of which around 2,000 have survived the centuries, forming one of the most remarkable architectural legacies in Southeast Asia and serving as the country's foremost cultural attraction. Travelling around in a horse cart (Image), we also visited some of the finest

lacquerware artists (Image) and even purchased a large lacquerware chest that still adorns my living room today. In any case, nowhere else have I seen such a concentration of sacred architecture, and Bagan left an indelible impression on us. It is a place without equal.

We also took the opportunity to once again visit the Shwedagon Pagoda in Yangon, which I had already seen as a young man during my tour around the world. Again, it exuded the same unique atmosphere of sacredness, grandeur, and luminance that it did back when I first visited it in 1973. This golden temple is to Burmese Buddhists what the Kaaba is for Muslims and the St. Peter's Basilica for Roman Catholics (Image: Shwedagon Pagode by night).

In February of 1992, I made my first visit to *PAPUA NEW GUINEA* (PNG)—the eastern half of New Guinea, the second-largest island in the world after Greenland. PNG is a land of immense cultural and ethnic diversity. The Papuans – ethnicities with dark skin and curly hair – remain divided into countless tribes, clans, and family groups, each with their particular customs, traditions, and languages. Until recently, they had had no written script as yet.

Though significantly reduced in recent years, tribal warfare still persisted. In fact, during my visit, I witnessed a village gathering, armed with clubs and sticks, preparing to engage a neighboring clan. In many ways, the Papuans had been thrust directly from the Stone Age into the digital era. Some of the highland tribes—living in the rugged central mountains—made their "first contact" with outsiders only in the 1950s. At a time when their world extended no further than the horizon where the clouds met the earth, and when metal tools or the wheel were as yet unknown to them, they were suddenly confronted with airplanes, electricity, machine guns, motor vehicles, money, and – Christianity.

Even at the time of my visit, the transition remained jarring. Concepts like bank accounts, financial remittances, and audited reports were foreign and often misunderstood. Many local organizations struggled to produce proper documentation or to account for the use of donated funds. My staff back at the German office had sometimes complained that their letters were not answered and project reports from PNG were late in coming – if they came at all. In addressing that problem, one indigenous person told me: "We normally relate to each other not by writing letters but by touching another's hands and arms."

Ironically, the underdeveloped state of the country also presented a rare opportunity. In Papua New Guinea, it was still possible to introduce services for people with disabilities without repeating the earlier mistakes of expensive institutionalization. From the outset, one could promote community-based rehabilitation (CBR) and inclusive education. The PNG people showed openness to these progressive ideas, yet successful implementation still required salaried staff, solid organization, and strong leadership—qualities that were not widely developed in the region.

CBM was supporting six programs for people with disabilities across the country. In Port Moresby, the capital, I visited the local Association for the

Blind, the National Board for Disabled Persons, and a Special Education Center. From there, I traveled to the central regions, visiting programs in Lae, Madang, Wewak, Goroka, and Mount Hagen. The highland region is mostly covered by tropical rainforest and rugged terrain, making it difficult to develop a transportation infrastructure. More than 1000 ethnic groups exist in PNG, and many cultural expressions have emerged. Most of these tribes have their own language. People of the highlands engage in diverse rituals, adorning and painting themselves colorfully.

In Mt. Hagen, I visited a hospital where we hoped to initiate an eye care program. Overall, the country's national program for the prevention of blindness was still in its infancy. But there was considerable potential for growth—with proper training, resources, and commitment, much could be achieved. It was a place to which I would have to return again.

In May, I made yet another trip to **CHINA** for which I invited two outstanding Thai professionals to accompany me: Dr. Soontorn Antarasena, Chief ENT Surgeon at the Bangkok Central Hospital, and Dr. Maliwan Tammasaeng, Principal of the Bangkok School for the Deaf. Their expertise in audiology and education for the deaf, respectively, proved invaluable in helping me evaluate the projects we visited. Alongside us was Mrs. Gu Xiuhui from the Amity Foundation in Nanjing—CBM's trusted partner organization in China. Her contributions were indispensable, not only offering Amity's perspective on the projects but also serving as our interpreter, as most of our contacts in China spoke little or no English (Image).

Our journey began with a flight from Bangkok to Beijing, where we visited, among other places, a rehabilitation center for deaf children. There we met the remarkable Mrs. Wan Xuanrong, whose personal story had led her to become a pioneer in speech training. She had taught her son, born deaf, to speak and lip-read, in addition to learning sign language. Drawing on her own personal experiences, she went on to establish a rehabilitation center and championed a more integrated, speech-focused approach to deaf education in China. Entirely self-taught, Mrs. Wan had become an inspiration and an asset to the national effort to support children with hearing loss.

We learned that China was home to more than 700,000 deaf children under the age of seven—a staggering figure that underscored the urgency of the work ahead. We also met Dr. Deng Yuancheng, head of the prestigious Beijing ENT Institute and a key influence on Mrs. Wan. He was widely respected as a pioneer in his field and offered valuable insights into the medical causes of deafness in China. Chief among them, he explained, was ototoxicity—a damaging side effect of certain medications. Meningitis, too, remained a major contributor.

While still in Beijing, we took a brief break from our official duties to visit some of China's iconic historical landmarks. We toured the famous Ming Tombs, where thirteen emperors of the Ming Dynasty (1368–1644) lie buried in a grand necropolis that draws millions of visitors each year. The site stands as a testament to the enduring richness of traditional Chinese culture and imperial legacy.

No visit to northern China would be complete without seeing the Great Wall (Image: Dr. Maliwan and Kurt at the Chinese Wall). Begun as early as the 7th century BC, the Chinese Wall spans over 20,000 kilometers and remains one of the most awe-inspiring architectural feats in human history. We climbed a section of it and walked a few hundred meters along its ancient stones, mar-

veling at both its scale and symbolism. At a nearby tourist stall, I discovered a beautifully crafted Samurai sword—ornate, well-balanced, and surprisingly affordable. I purchased it as a gift for Patrick and had it carefully packed into a box to check in as luggage.

We next traveled to Wuhan, in central China—a city now widely known as the origin of the coronavirus pandemic. At the time of our visit, however, Wuhan was notable to us not only for its Crane Tower (Image), but also for its commitment to deaf education. We visited the "No. 2 School for the Deaf," which, despite its name, was widely regarded as the leading school for the deaf in Hubei Province.

We had also planned to visit the Wuhan School for the Blind, but unfortunately, I fell severely ill with the flu and a high fever. Thankfully, Dr. Soontorn was provided me with medical treatment, and I recovered quickly enough to complete the remainder of our journey.

While in Wuhan, we also met with the staff of the Institute of Child Health Care, a multifaceted institution engaged in research, training, prevention, screening, diagnosis, and treatment. The issue of hearing impairment figured prominently in their work. Here, deafness was viewed through the lens of epidemiology—recognized as a largely preventable condition. Infections of the middle ear were cited as a leading cause of hearing loss, particularly in children. It was encouraging to see the growing awareness that early detection and medical intervention could mitigate many cases of avoidable deafness.

From Wuhan, we continued on to Nanjing for further discussions with our partner organization, the Amity Foundation, and to visit the Special Education Teachers Training School—an institution CBM had been actively supporting for several years. This center played a critical role in training special educators from across China. At the time of our visit, the school had around 1,000 students enrolled, with 400 of them specializing in hearing impairment.

While in Nanjing, we also visited a school for deaf-mute children, a hearing rehabilitation center, and a school for the blind. At the People's Hospital of Jiangsu Province, I was invited to deliver the opening remarks for an optometry training course led by Dr. C. Parker, an experienced American optometrist. The course brought together eye doctors from various provinces across China and aimed to enhance their ability to prescribe and fit eyeglasses correctly—a much-needed skill in many parts of the country.

During the visit, we also toured the hospital's large ophthalmology department. There, I met a patient who had recently undergone a corneal graft after losing his sight due to severe burns. His case was a reminder of the impact timely medical intervention can have on someone's quality of life.

From Nanjing, we flew to Changsha, the capital of Hunan Province, where we visited a school for the deaf and blind as well as the Hunan Provincial People's Hospital to assess its ophthalmology department.

From Changsha, we flew west to Chengdu, the capital of Sichuan Province. Sichuan is the largest of the Chinese provinces, similar to Spain in size, and to Germany in terms of population. We visited the School for the Blind and Deaf, as well as the West China University of Medical Sciences, which I had previously toured during my first visit there with Dr. Norval Christy.

While it was my second visit to the ophthalmology department, it was our first visit to the ENT department. We met with the university's President and the director of the ENT department, both of whom welcomed us warmly.

We also visited the Sichuan Provincial Hospital in Chengdu, where we met Dr. Zhang Guohui, the chief ophthalmologist, and Dr. Lo Wen-Bin, a retired pioneer in ophthalmology. Dr. Lo left a lasting impression on us with his vast experience, kind nature, and lifelong dedication to eye care services. As a gesture of goodwill, he presented me with an old portable slit lamp of his own design, originally created for use by rural doctors in underserved areas. I still keep it as a reminder of that visit.

Additionally, we met Dr. Ting, the hospital's chief ENT doctor. To gain a deeper understanding of the structure and challenges of the Chinese health-care system, we extended our visits beyond the provincial capital and toured several rural health facilities. These included a county hospital in Erbian County, a township hospital in Xihe, and a small village dispensary. At the

dispensary, we met a local "doctor" who, in reality, was at best a basic health worker with limited training. She had never heard of cataracts and would not have been able to recognize one even if she saw one. It was an example of how underdeveloped some rural regions still were at the time.

We also made a small stop in Leshan, where we visited the world's largest Sitting Buddha carved out of a cliff face of Cretaceous red sandstone near the confluence of the Min River and the Duda River. Being more than 70 meters high (233 ft), the Leshan Giant Buddha was constructed between 723 to 803 AD (Image). When seen from a ship, the mountain range where the

Buddha is located, appears to be shaped like a slumbering Buddha (Image). It is for that reason that the locals say, "The mountain is a Buddha, and the Buddha is a mountain."

Finally, we travelled—if I recall correctly, by train—to Kunming, a city I had visited before. This time, we paid visits to the School for the Deaf and Blind and the Provincial Red Cross Hospital. From Kunming, we returned to Bangkok, where I thanked my two highly competent companions, Dr. Soontorn and the gracious Dr. Maliwan. Their expertise had been invaluable in assessing the projects we visited, and their recommendations proved extremely useful in shaping future CBM support.

Our trip revealed a country at a pivotal moment—on the verge of opening itself to the Western world, eager to learn from leading international experts, and determined to improve its services for the deaf and blind. During my first visit to China I had still sensed that many Chinese wanted to visit the U.S., hoping for a good career. But during this most recent trip, people told me that this was the time for them to stay in China as their country was offering so many opportunities for development and career possibilities.

The hospitality and friendliness of the people we visited in China was more than generous. In one case, we were even greeted with a student concert (Image). And frequently we were invited by our Chinese hosts to a lavish

dinner with numerous courses – typically with a rotating tray (called Lazy Susan) placed on top of the table for easy access to the different food dishes. At the end of the dinner, we were invited to a liqueur that we had to drink "bottoms up" (or "Ganbei", as the Chinese say) (Image).

On a later trip to Bangkok, when Aline joined me, we invited Dr. Soontorn, the ENT surgeon, for an evening dinner to reflect on our journey through China and discuss

the evolving situation in the country. Our conversation also turned to the many unusual foods we had sampled during the many meals with our hospitable Chinese friends: frog legs, snakes, scorpions, turtles, and a variety of other exotic dishes. I casually remarked that "the only thing I hadn't eaten in China was dog meat." To my surprise, Dr. Soontorn corrected me, saying that we had, in fact, eaten dog meat in Kunming. Looking back, I was relieved I hadn't realized it at the time.

As for that last trip to China, I must recount what happened when I finally arrived back home. As I flew from Bangkok to Malaysia and arrived at Penang Airport, I collected my checked-in luggage, cleared immigration, and proceeded toward customs. I stopped to pause for a moment, fearing that I might have problems with the Samurai sword I had purchased near the Chinese Wall. Recalling what had happened when Patrick had bought a spear in Indonesia which the Penang customs confiscated, I began to worry about what they would do with that narrow Chinese box. While customs officers in Penang usually waved through personal luggage without much argument, they were always suspicious of tourist boxes—especially anything out of the ordinary. They would want to know what was in it. Would they confiscate it again? What should I tell them?

I considered the fact that while customs officers typically spoke decent English, they weren't always familiar with a more nuanced and sophisticated vocabulary. When one of the officers eventually asked me what was inside the box, I replied calmly, "Oh, it's a replica of a Chinese artefact." He looked at me blankly for a moment, perhaps unsure of what I'ld meant, but then nodded politely, as though he understood, and waved me through without another word. I breathed a sigh of relief. The gift had made it through customs, and I was able to present the sword to Patrick when I arrived home—much to his delight.

In July 1992, I attended a WHO workshop on Low Vision in Bangkok (Image), followed shortly by the Asian Congress on Deafness, also held in Bangkok. Then, in September, I travelled to Germany to participate in CBM's Executive Meeting and to take part in budget discussions.

In November, I flew to *AUSTRALIA* for the first time, to attend a regional workshop on the prevention of blindness that took place in the beautiful city of Sydney. The event was organized by the World Health Organization (WHO) and the International Agency for the Prevention of Blindness (IAPB). These conferences, attended by invitees from Southeast Asia and the Pacific, offered opportunities for insightful conversations and professional exchange. CBM's efforts in the region were frequently referenced, acknowledged, and appreciated throughout the event.

119

While in Sydney, I took the opportunity to explore the city and found this metropolis to be one of the finest in the world. Strolling through the vibrant city center, I eventually settled down for dinner at a charming German-Australian restaurant, where I was served the most delicious onion soup I had ever eaten recall. Whenever I eat onion soup, it has to measure up against the one I enjoyed at that restaurant. While in Sydney, I also took the opportunity to enjoy a scenic boat ride around the Sydney Harbour near the iconic Opera House.

At the workshop I teamed up with Dr. Joseph Taylor, a CBM eye doctor and highly valued consultant with whom I had agreed to travel to some of the Pacific islands after the event. From Sydney, we flew to the small island nation of *TONGA*, where we visited a Red Cross Center for people with various disabilities, but their services were very basic, and there was little expertise available. In many cases, disabled children were left without any intervention at all. One of our considerations was to send experts to Tonga to help improve these services. We also visited the hospital, which had an eye department, and spoke with the ophthalmologist in charge, then also with an ENT doctor, and, finally, with the government's Director of Health.

Next, we flew to *WESTERN SAMOA*, an island nation consisting of two major islands. We visited three CBM-supported projects in and around Apia, the capital city: the National Society for the Disabled, the Western Samoa Society for the Intellectually Handicapped, and a program focused on the prevention of blindness and the rehabilitation of the blind. We met with staff and board members from these organizations to assess their progress and challenges.

Dr. Taylor and I stayed at a simple, yet charming hotel near the beach, run by an American couple whose story intrigued me. They had left behind successful careers as lawyers in the U.S. as they wanted to escape the stressfulness and anxieties of American life and enjoy a slower pace of living. After making a long list of potential destinations and weighing their respective pros and cons, they eventually settled on Western Samoa for its climate, beaches, and relaxed way of life. With their savings, they built a tourist hotel, which was unfortunately devastated by a typhoon shortly after its completion. However, they decided to rebuild it right away, and we were able to enjoy their lovely establishment.

From Apia, we flew to Suva, the capital of *FIJI*, primarily to address an important administrative issue affecting the Fiji Society for the Blind (FSB). CBM and other donor organizations had suspended their funding until certain managerial problems would have been solved. A number of people I had spoken to repeatedly pointed to the Secretary of the Governing Board as the main source of FSB's problems. His erratic and dictatorial behavior interfered with day-to-day operations, making it difficult to effectively run the institution. I was determined to resolve the issue.

120

On our first morning in Fiji, I met with the department heads to discuss the programs and ongoing challenges. They, once again, voiced serious concerns about the Board Secretary, whom I had previously invited to have lunch with. During our meal, I first sought to establish a friendly rapport with him, but then I asked him if I was correct in assuming he was truly the leading figure of the society. When he confirmed my assumption, I addressed the many problems for which the financial support had been withheld, explaining that I considered him to be responsible for them, and I requested his resignation. Although he was obviously both astounded and offended by my request, he eventually reassured me that he would not seek re-election during the upcoming Board elections, which I considered an acceptable solution.

Later that day, Dr. Taylor and I attended the FSB Board meeting, where we also addressed the current state of affairs. We asked the Board to take full responsibility for all the ongoing issues. I didn't mention my earlier meeting with the Secretary in which I had requested his resignation, and neither did he. It was a face-saving course of action. In a letter to me later, the Secretary informed me that he had not stood for re-election but intended to apply for a seat in Fiji's parliament. This experience highlighted a recurring challenge I have encountered over the years: Many of the problems in project management were not necessarily due to a lack of expertise, but lack of managerial and leadership skills.

Our final stop on this journey was the *SOLOMON ISLANDS*, where the Health Ministry had requested CBM to send an eye doctor. A visit to the eye department of the Central Hospital in Honiara confirmed the urgent need for such support. Many patients were waiting for surgery. From Honiara, the capital city, we flew back to Sydney, and then returned home.

In January 1993, I was invited to *INDIA* to attend a workshop on managing eye-care delivery, organized by the World Health Organization. The training took place at the renowned Aravind Eye Hospital in Madurai in the very south of the subcontinent. As the workshop was to last five days, I decided to bring Aline and Patrick along, giving them the opportunity to experience a glimpse of India while I sat "in class."

On our journey to Madurai, we stopped in Madras—now Chennai—and Tiruchirappalli. In Tiruchirappalli, we were welcomed by CBM's Regional Director for India, who had two assistance, one of whom invited us to his home, where he introduced us to his strikingly beautiful daughter of whom he was obviously very proud. The subject turned to the problem of the bride dowry which in India the parents of a bride have to pay to the groom when they get married. We learned that this family had been saving up for decades in order to be able to pay the enormous dowry. We were even told the expected amount to be paid in rupiah. I compared that to the father's presumed salary and concluded that if I had to pay a similar amount in dollars, given my own salary, the dowry would be tantamount to saving up for a house in Germany. I asked myself: Was the dowry good or bad? At least, I thought, the newly-wed couple would have a substantial sum of money with which to start their marriage.

In our hotel in Madurai, where the workshop took place, we encountered a Greek professor of physics. He struck up a conversation with Patrick, who was already a promising student in the subject and leaning toward a future in the sciences. The professor passionately recommended to him the famous *Feynman Lectures on Physics*. Inspired by the encounter, we later searched for and found a printed edition of these lectures in Bangalore—locally published and very reasonably priced. Patrick was thrilled. That spark lit by a chance meeting would eventually grow into a deeper passion, leading him to eventually pursue studies in both Physics and Mathematics.

In Bangalore, we also visited the impressive Legislative House (Image: Vidhana Soudha), before moving on to the city of Mysore where we saw the Jaganmohana Palace which also serves as an Art Gallery (Image: Jaganmohana). It was thrillig to take in the rich tapestry of the region.

On another journey to **INDIA** (I cannot even remember when it was), I was scheduled to attend a workshop in New Delhi, and once again, I invited Aline to join me, while Patrick had to attend school. After the workshop, we set off to explore the celebrated landscapes of Rajasthan in Northwest India where ancient forts rise like mirages from the desert. In Jaipur we visited the pink-hued "Palace of the Winds," and in Jodhpur we could admire the Umaid Bhawan Palace, the Mandore Garden and the Mehrangarh Castle (Images opposite page). Each place offered its own rhythm, its own glitter, its own legend.

From there, we continued our journey to Agra, where the ethereal beauty of the Taj Mahal left us awestruck once again—its marble silhouette shifting hues with the changing light (Images). Finally, we reached Varanasi, the

123

spiritual heart of India, where the Ganges flows in solemn grace, thousands of devotees bathe in its holy water (Image), and burial rituals unfold along the ghats as they have for centuries. Here, where people from all over India display their most exotic characters (Image), we also saw the Dhamek Stupa again (cf. p. 57) where Buddha gave his first teaching. I had visited these places during my round-the-world tour as a young man, but now I was happy to share these sites with Aline who was equally impressed as I had been.

These journeys were a vivid reminder of India's astonishing cultural and architectural richness—its multi-ethnic, multilingual vibrancy, and the astonishing array of fortresses, palaces, and temples that speak of dynasties past and spiritual traditions still very much alive. These were voyages through time and spirit, that deepened our appreciation for the sheer complexity and beauty of this ancient land.

Back home at the office, I could not linger there for long as my next trip took me again to *INDONESIA* in collaboration with Dr. Joe Taylor, CBM's ophthalmic consultant. In February 2023, we traveled to Jakarta, where we met with the head of the eye department at the University of Indonesia. We also spoke with the Director of the Rural Eye Program at the Department of Health and learned that 2,000 of the country's 6,000 rural health centers provide primary eye care services. CBM was asked to assist with the local production of eye drops.

We then flew to *IRIAN JAYA*, the Indonesian part of New Guinea, which has a very scattered population. A total of 200 languages are spoken in Irian Jaya, most of which have no written script. With vast stretches of untouched forest and almost no roads to speak of, air travel was our only means of getting around. Flying in a twin engine airplane (Image), our first stop was at Wamena, located in the central highlands, where it was customary for some of the tribes to mummify some of their dead. In fact, in one village, we were proudly presented with one such a mummified ancestor (Image). Here in Wamena, we visited Wamena Hospital which was run by two Christian Indonesian doctors. From there, we flew to remote Mulia in the middle of the

jungle, where we landed on a relatively short grass airstrip. We visited the small hospital here, which CBM had been supporting for a number of years, and Dr. Taylor conducted an outpatient eye clinic there.

Most people in Irian Jaya still lived in ways that hadn't changed for thousands of years. They resided in the simplest of circumstances, with women wearing straw skirts and men donning their traditional penis gourds. Many men also wore large boar tusks through their noses. Most tribes lived in round huts covered with straw, without any windows (Image). To stay warm,

they made fires in the center of their huts, with the smoke filling the air, making it somewhat difficult to breathe. Until very recently, most of the indigenous population had lived in the Stone Age; and many inland Papuans still preserve their original cultures and customs, which vary somewhat between the different ethnic groups. Any cultural anthropologist visiting this region would have an excellent field day.

After our visits to the highlands, we flew back to Sentani, then to Jakarta, and finally home to Penang.

In April 1993, I had to make yet another trip to *CHINA*, this time limited to Nanjing, where I held extensive discussions with the staff of the Amity Foundation and attended a workshop with CBM project partners. The two-day workshop brought together 45 participants from across China. The training provided another excellent opportunity to speak directly with many of our partners about their training plans and other ongoing or proposed developments. As always, I documented my visit thoroughly, writing a comprehensive report detailing all the individuals I met with and the topics discussed, particularly regarding training and future development plans.

The next trip, in May 1993, took me back to **VIETNAM**, where I attended an NGO meeting in Hanoi organized by the World Health Organization in collaboration with the University of Medicine in Tokyo and the University of Melbourne—both recognized WHO collaborating centers for the prevention of blindness. Since the trip was limited to Hanoi, I invited Aline to join me and to explore the city while I attended the conference. She gladly accepted and spent her time sightseeing and shopping in Hanoi.

The first day of the workshop was reserved exclusively for NGOs, while the second day included participants of the Vietnamese Ministry of Health. One of the topics discussed was the growing trend in Vietnam to introduce intraocular lenses (IOLs) following cataract surgery, moving away from the traditional approach of simply removing the cloudy lens and providing the patient with spectacles. Until then, this simpler method had also been CBM's official policy, as it was more affordable and accessible in most low-income countries. However, given the increased funding with which several NGOs were prepared to support Vietnam, as well as the decreasing cost of IOLs, the transition toward implanting artificial lenses appeared both feasible and desirable.

At the time, two primary methods were in use for IOL placement: inserting the artificial lens into the anterior chamber (between the cornea and the iris), or into the posterior chamber (behind the iris, in front of the lens capsule). The latter method had proven to be safer and was increasingly adopted by trained eye surgeons. With surgical techniques improving and lens costs dropping, it was agreed that, at least in Vietnam, IOLs should become the standard procedure wherever qualified surgeons were available.

The workshop concluded with a gala dinner, hosted by the Minister of Health, to thank all participants. However, I chose to spend the evening with Aline instead, since we had had little time together during the conference. We enjoyed a quiet dinner for two at our hotel. Meanwhile, during the gala, the Minister of Health looked for me in order to present me with a gift as a token of appreciation for CBM's support over the years. Upon discovering I wasn't there, he excused himself from the dinner and came personally to our hotel. I apologized for my absence, but he warmly assured me it was no problem, and handed me the gift. I felt deeply honored by his kind gesture and by his willingness to go out of his way to express his gratitude.

After carefully considering all the arguments regarding intraocular lenses, that had been exchanged at the Hanoi conference, I drafted a policy paper titled "Time for Change" and submitted it to CBM headquarters. Initially, it was met with only lukewarm interest, if not open criticism. However, over the following months and years, CBM's policy gradually shifted, and we began to support cataract surgeries with intraocular lens implants whenever feasible.

Not long after, CBM ophthalmologist Dr. Albrecht Henning emerged as a true pioneer in this regard. In Pokhara, Nepal, he introduced a model he had previously observed in Taxila, setting up four operating tables and moving swiftly from one to the next, performing cataract surgeries and implanting intraocular lenses in most patients. The results were outstanding.

What many people in Western countries do not realize is that, in low-income countries, especially in rural regions, millions of individuals still live in the dark—both literally and figuratively—with regard to cataract blindness. They often do not know that this form of blindness is easily curable. As a result, many have gone needlessly blind, with devastating consequences for their personal lives, independence, and social integration. One of CBM's key goals has been to raise awareness—both among healthcare providers and the general public—so that when people develop a cataract, they understand it is treatable and know where to seek medical therapy.

Of course, not all forms of blindness—or deafness, for that matter—are curable. In such cases, the focus must shift from medical treatment to rehabilitation and education. Blind children, for instance, should no longer be left idly at home, hidden away from society, as has often been the custom for generations. Instead, they can be taught to read braille, learn orientation and mobility skills, and gain a large measure of independence. Today, a wide range of assistive technologies—such as screen readers and refreshable braille displays—enable blind individuals to read documents, surf the internet, and perform almost any task a sighted person can do.

Similarly, deaf individuals are not only taught sign language to communicate with their peers, but also oral language, enabling them to engage in conversation with hearing people. In addition, they are trained to lip-read, helping them understand what others are saying even in the absence of sound.

The overarching goal is to integrate people with disabilities as fully as possible into everyday life, ensuring that their physical impairment does not limit their ability to participate in the same activities as everyone else. A disability should not automatically render someone "disabled" in the broader sense of the word. In many ways, disability is less about the individual's condition but more about the barriers that society places in their way—through exclusion, segregation, or lack of accommodation. True disability arises not from the impairment itself, but from society's failure to include and empower.

In June 1993, I made another visit to *CAMBODIA*. CBM Headquarters had requested that I assess both the national eye care program and a community-based rehabilitation (CBR) initiative. Before meeting with our partner organizations, I took the opportunity to privately fly to Siem Reap in the northwest of the country, to visit magnificent Angkor Wat and to explore the many temples and ancient ruins in the area, some of which were partly reclaimed by nature, overgrown with trees and dense vegetation. Angkor Wat is Cambodia's national pride and truly one of the wonders of the world. Its sheer scale, symmetry, and grandeur are awe-inspiring, with intricate stone carvings depicting scenes from Hindu mythology adorning its walls (Images).

It was not only the grandeur of Angkor Wat that stirred the soul, but also the scattered temples and crumbling ruins that surround it—some worn by time, others gently reclaimed by wild, unbridled growth (Image). Wandering among them, I felt as though I had stumbled upon sacred relics the world had nearly forgotten. Not to be polished or restored, but cherished precisely as they are: timeless echoes of human hands entwined with the quiet persistence of nature.

But my visit to Angkor Wat was not just about ancient archeological sites. There also was a human side to it. As I stood at the foot of the grand staircase leading up to the temple complex, I encountered a young begging boy who had been blinded by a landmine. Nothing was being done for him at the time, and meeting him brought home the urgent need to provide services for Cambodia's blind population and those injured or disabled by landmines.

Returning to Phnom Penh, I visited a community-based rehabilitation program for the blind, initiated by Maryknoll, a U.S.-based organization that runs several programs for people with disabilities in Cambodia. One of the key questions we discussed was whether the program should continue focusing solely on blindness or expand to include individuals with other types of disabilities. Given the principles behind the CBR model, I felt that a cross-disability approach would be more effective and inclusive.

In June 1993, my next trip took me once again to *JAVA*, Indonesia's main island. I was accompanied for part of the journey by CBM co-worker Nicola Crews. Our first stop was the Jakarta office of Helen Keller International. We also visited the Christian University in Jakarta and its eye department. Next, we went to see the Rawinala School for multihandicapped blind children. We continued our journey to Surabaya, where we visited the eye department at Airlangga University, which CBM had been supporting for some time.

From there, we traveled to hospitals in Malang and Mojowarno, and moved on to visit a diaconal service of the Javanese Church, which provided support for blind individuals. We then moved on to a community-based Development and Training Center in Solo, which had gained considerable recognition for its work. Our final stop was in Yogyakarta, where we visited a rehabilitation center that had recently become a CBM partner.

In June 1993, I travelled once again to *BURMA* (now Myanmar), visiting several projects in Yangon on my first day there. The next day began with a visit to the German Ambassador to Burma, followed by a tour of some government-run initiatives.

On the third day, I made a journey to Myitkyina in northern Myanmar. Although CBM had been supporting a small school for the blind there for a good number of years, no CBM staff had ever visited the place, as foreign travel to that region was generally restricted. We flew with an old Fokker 27 twin-propeller plane operated by Myanmar Airways—an airline that hardly inspired much confidence. I was accompanied by U Thein Lwin, the blind but able school director from Yangon, who was also the driving force behind the Myitkyina project.

Foreigners were generally barred from visiting Myitkyina due to an ongoing insurgency involving two warring local armies. My visit became possible only because I had, metaphorically speaking, "danced with the devil": I had cultivated a friendly relationship with the dictatorial government, namely the Director General of the Welfare Department, with whom I had dined the night before. He issued an official invitation, which gave me the rare privilege of accessing this otherwise restricted region. Upon arrival, I had to register with a local government official. I asked him: "How many European visitors have been here over the past few years?" He replied, without hesitation:

"You are the first—and the last."

Despite its population of 160,000, the city of Myitkyina felt more like a backward village. Electricity was scarce, available only two or three days a week. Nearby was a jade-mining area, where a lucky find could make you rich overnight. But Myitkyina, the capital of Myanmar's Kachin State, was also notorious for its drug problems—heroin and opium abuse being rampant, with an estimated 50,000 addicts.

Since there was no hotel in Myitkyina, we were accommodated in a private home with no hot water, and in fact, no running water at all. I didn't mind bathing with cold water, but the absence of running water and missing a proper shower was always a personal challenge for me. For my Burmese travel companion it was no problem at all. They could accomodate for that.

We visited the school for the blind, which had 32 students spread across five classes. By almost any standard, the school was very basic and of low quality. Nonetheless, the children were learning essential life skills and receiving a basic education—an important step toward a more independent life.

During our stay, we also met with the General Secretary of the Kachin Baptist Convention (Image). He spoke at length about the severe medical needs in the region, particularly in the rural areas. He appealed to us to send an eye doctor to Kachin State, as not a single ophthalmologist was available in the entire region.

Another visit took us to the Kachin Theological College, a Baptist seminary with 257 students. The President of the college invited me to speak to students and staff—most of whom had never seen a white person like me before. My visit seemed to bring them a sense of hope that perhaps, with international attention, some things might begin to change for the better. The seminary itself lacked even the most basic amenities—no electricity, no running water, and few of the conveniences we normally take for granted.

Upon our return to Rangoon, we embarked on a seven-hour drive south to Moulmein—another part of the country that, like Myitkyina, was typically closed off to outsiders. There, we visited a leprosy hospital and a feeding program that allowed children to attend school. CBM had supported this program for several years. We returned to Rangoon the same day. On our final day in the country, we paid a visit to the Anglican Archbishop before catching our return flight to Bangkok.

This marked the end of my assignment on behalf of the Bangkok office. With the Regional Director of the Penang office retiring, I was now set to take over his role. The Penang office oversaw CBM-supported projects in Malaysia, Indonesia, the Philippines, and the Pacific. But while we had very much enjoyed living in Penang, it made strategic sense to relocate the office to the Philippines, where the majority of CBM-supported projects in the region were based.

Mastering Manila

We began searching for office and residential space in Manila and eventually rented a house in the Bel Air district of Makati where we could live and have our office, too. Our belongings were shipped over to Manila, and we prepared to settle into our new home.

The move came at an opportune time for Patrick who had become increasingly dissatisfied with the quality of the American school he was attending in Penang. When we informed him about the move to Manila, he was enthusiastic—especially upon learning that the Philippine capital had an excellent International School. We relocated sometime between July and August, just in time for Patrick to start the new school year.

The first weeks in Manila were extremely busy for all of us. Patrick had to adjust to life at the International School. Aline was occupied with unpacking and arranging our furnitures once they had arrived via container ship. As for me, I was tasked with setting up the new office, interviewing and hiring staff—all while maintaining regular correspondence with our project partners and CBM headquarters. It was probably the busiest period of my life, with work stretching around the clock for weeks on end.

We also had to purchase a car to get around the city, hire a driver, and slowly begin to figure out where things were in Manila. Compared to my very first visit to Makati back in 1973, the city had grown enormously, and the population surge had brought with it almost unbearable traffic congestion. A large shopping complex nearby—the Mega Mall—was just seven minutes away if traffic was clear. But in most cases it took us an hour to get there, often only to discover that all parking spaces were full and we had to return empty-handed. The Mega Mall wasn't just a shopping destination; it also had twelve cinemas showing the latest Hollywood films for as little as a dollar per person. Unfortunately, we rarely took advantage of that, due to the traffic and my relentless workload.

For Patrick, the International School turned out to be a real blessing. He enjoyed most of his teachers, adapted well to the classroom environment, and even fell in love with a lovely girl from Bangladesh who helped him adjust to the new setting (Image: Patrick and Famida).

As for me, I was so overwhelmed with work that I barely had time to check in with myself emotionally. Aline, however, had a much harder time adjusting. She constantly com-

pared life in Manila to the more relaxed, scenic lifestyle she had enjoyed in Penang. Penang had been a beautiful, manageable island with easy access to beaches and outdoor spaces. Manila, in contrast, was a sprawling metropolis of some 14 million people, plagued with endless traffic jams and little room for nature or leisure.

To compensate for this new reality, Aline insisted we get a dog. We found a beautiful Afghan hound with a light cream coat and a curled ringtail (Image: Amadeo). On weekends, when we wanted to go for a longer walk, the only place we could reliably go to was a Filipino cemetery—a rather unusual, but peaceful place to stretch our legs and find a bit of calm.

After some months, when the heaviest workload had been managed, I could relax somewhat and even decided to paint a bit. Years earlier, during a vacation in what was then Yugoslavia, I had encountered an excellent portrait artist and persuaded Aline to sit for a painting. As I observed the artist at work and asked him about his materials, I thought to myself, *I can do that too.* I started painting in pastels, but here in Manila I transitioned to oils (Image). But time was scarce, and there was always something urgent to do around the house or the office. I also had to familiarize myself with the CBM-supported projects in the Philippines.

Most people in Manila spoke at least some English, in addition to Tagalog, the daily vernacular among locals. Educated Filipinos typically spoke and wrote excellent English. However, the majority of them—such as shop assistants or taxi drivers—communicated in a simpler form of English, often unaware of the finer nuances and subtleties the language holds. Aline found this quite frustrating, as she often failed to make herself understood – along with many other challenges that made adjusting to life in Manila difficult for her. She experienced a full-blown culture shock here, further exacerbated by the fact that she had little to do that offered a sense of recognition or accomplishment.

While we were still settling into our home and setting up the office, I embarked on my first tour of duty in December 1993, which took me to Davao City in the South of the Philippines, then on to North Sulawesi (which is part of Indonesia), and finally to Denpasar on the island of Bali.

In *DAVAO CITY* I visited a community-based rehabilitation program that included an eye care component. Under this program, patients were screened and referred for treatment or surgery if needed. I then visited another agricultural rehabilitation and prevention of blindness program. A further visit took me to a training center for the physically handicapped—established by a Catholic sister, Dr. Cecilia Wood, whose work was yet another testament to the remarkable contributions of Catholic sisters across the globe.

133

I hadn't booked a hotel in Davao City, assuming it would be easy to find accommodation upon arrival. To my surprise all hotels in the city were fully booked. I was told, however, that one resort on nearby Samal Island still had rooms available. So I took a ferry across the Davao Gulf to reach the Pearl Farm Beach Resort on Samal Island's eastern shore—and was absolutely flabbergasted by the sheer beauty of the place (Image).

To this day, I consider it the most charming resort I have ever stayed at. I was assigned a room built directly above the ocean water, where I could dangle my legs from the balcony and watch the fish swimming below. Just ahead was a small, palm-covered tiny island—so perfectly picturesque that it felt almost surreal, like something out of a cheap kitschy picture postcard. The pool at the resort was cleverly designed to appear as though it flowed directly into the sea.

Apart from sunbathing and swimming, eating and drinking, there wasn't much else to do on the island, so guests were essentially confined to the resort itself—but what a place to be confined to! I made a firm resolution then and there to return one day with Aline and enjoy proper holidays together in this tropical paradise.

Returning to Davao City the next day, I flew to Manado, located at the northern tip of **SULAWESI**—one of Indonesia's larger islands. There, a new community-based program was about to be launched, and support had been requested from CBM. I also visited a primary eye care program in the Minahasa District that CBM had already been supporting. I encouraged the local doctors to expand their services beyond their district, as the need throughout the province remained enormous.

Minahasa is known for its traditional houses, which feature a distinctive architectural style. These homes are built on stilts made of ironwood, which hardens with time to become as strong as iron. The space beneath the houses is typically used for storing crops. Often, two staircases flank the house, leading up to a front porch and the main living areas (Image opposite page).

My final stop on this trip was Denpasar, the main city on the island of **BALI**. I visited a mobile eye clinic (a Mazda van) which regularly travelled to various health centers on the island to conduct eye exams and perform surgeries. It was outfitted with an operating table and a microscope, enabling cataract operations to be performed directly on-site. Bali had a population of nearly three million, with an estimated 30,000 blind people—two-thirds of whom were blind due to cataracts. This meant that much of the blindness on the island could be prevented or reversed through this efficient mobile clinic. The project was now seeking funding from CBM and had submitted to us an official request.

Needless to say, Bali was a tourist destination of exceptional charm; it offered beautiful beaches, inviting hotels, unique shopping opportunities, exquisite artwork, and a rich Hindu culture found nowhere else in the Indonesian archipelago. I resolved to return one day for private holidays, together with Aline.

In January 1994, I teamed up once again with ophthalmologist Dr. Joseph Taylor for a trip to Jayapura in **IRIAN JAYA** on the island of New Guinea. We visited the Provincial Hospital and its eye department, and also paid a courtesy call to the hospital's director. From there, we flew to **NORTH SUMATRA** to visit Balige Hospital. Although we had previously sent one of their eye doctors to India for specialized training, the number of eye surgeries being performed remained disappointingly low. Several factors contributed to this underperformance: issues with church leadership, a light workload for the doctors, and an overall lack of commitment to the program.

We also visited the Hephata Center for the Blind and its adjacent community-based rehabilitation (CBR) program. Unfortunately, since the departure

of our dedicated co-worker Liz Cross, the quality and consistency of the CBR activities had noticeably deteriorated. Once again, I was reminded of a recurring truth in many developing countries: Progress is often slow and fragile. Development work faces persistent hurdles and obstacles—insufficient training, a shortage of qualified personnel, and a lack of administrative capacity; they all stand in the way of long-term success. My visits to CBM-supported projects was not always exciting and fulfilling, but at times, quite disappointing.

In May 1994, I flew again to **PAPUA NEW GUINEA**, where I visited a community-based rehabilitation (CBR) program in Port Moresby run by the Red Cross. I then traveled to Rabaul, located on the northern tip of New Britain—a separate island that forms part of the Bismarck Archipelago. In Rabaul, I visited a project for the disabled and a community-based rehabilitation program. Rabaul was known to be prone to earthquakes, and I experienced one while there. Although it was not high on the Richter scale, its epicenter was very close by, and I could clearly see my hotel swaying and the water in the pool rippling with the tremors.

From Rabaul, I flew to Lae, on the east coast of the main island, then to Goroka in the highlands and on to Madang and Wewak, both situated along the northern coast of PNG. In Wewak, I met Brother Graeme Leach, the dedicated leader of the Callan Services, as well as our CBM co-worker Sian Tesni from Wales, whom we had assigned there. Sian was an excellent expert in deafness and would later become a highly regarded global advisor for CBM. I continued my travel to Mt. Hagen, then to Mendi in the Southern Highlands; and finally flew back to Port Moresby before returning to Manila.

Back in Manila, I devoted much of my time visiting CBM-supported projects across the Philippines. Some were located in the greater Metro Manila area, in Baguio (Northern Luzon Peninsula), Bacolod City (Negros Island), Legazpi City (Southern Luzon), Tagbilaran (Bohol Island), and, of course, Davao City on the island of Mindanao. In February 1995, I returned once again to **INDONESIA**, beginning in Manado in North Sulawesi. From there, I traveled to Tana Toraja in West Sulawesi, and then on to Ujung Pandang (now known as Makassar) in South Sulawesi. Traveling to project sites in archipelagic nations like the Philippines and Indonesia meant hopping from island to island. Looking back, I have counted some 35 different islands I visited in total.

On a personal note, Aline and I also took time to enjoy some of the country's natural beauty, visiting the stunning beaches of Palawan Island and then returning to the delightful Pearl Farm Beach Resort on Samal Island where I had spend only one night before. We could both relish the paradise-like ambience, the clear ocean water, the good food, and each other's company.

As said before, I also had to travel to Germany twice a year for CBM's Executives' Meetings—once in March and once in September. I especially looked forward to the March meetings, because I cherished the refreshing spring air – after having endured the persistent heat and humidity of Southeast Asia. During these visits, I also came to appreciate the European seasons more than ever before—the changing temperatures, the lengthening and shortening of days, and the natural rhythm that defines life in Germany. In contrast, in places like Penang or Manila, the sun rises and sets almost at the same time every day, all year round. Over time, that constancy began to feel rather dull and monotonous, especially for Aline who did not have the privilege of visiting Germany twice a year, as I had.

In addition to her ongoing difficulties adjusting to life in the megacity of Manila, Aline experienced a deeply unfortunate and traumatic event—she was involved in a serious car accident. She had been out shopping and was sitting in the back of our Mazda 626, with our driver behind the wheel. As he turned left to cross a large, busy intersection, an oncoming bus—racing to beat the red light—crashed directly into the side of the car where Aline was seated. The impact was quite devastating. The car was completely totaled, and the bus driver fled the scene before he could be held accountable.

I received a call from a private Filipino gentleman who had witnessed the accident. He informed me that my wife had been injured and that he was taking her to the Makati Medical Center. I rushed to the hospital, where a doctor was removing glass splinters from Aline's face and body. After the procedure, the physician claimed she was fit to go home, stating there weren't any fractures. But it became immediately clear that something was seriously wrong—Aline couldn't walk. We had to place her in a wheelchair, and I hailed a taxi to take us home, where we gently helped her into bed.

Despite being home, Aline continued to suffer from intense pain. I called a local Filipino doctor to examine her. After a brief look, he dismissed her complaints, saying, "In a serious accident like that, some pain is to be expected." Because his casual assessment didn't sit right with me, I arranged for a German doctor to come to the house who had been practicing in Manila for many years. He asked Aline to pinpoint exactly where the pain was. When she indicated a specific spot on her pelvis, he applied slight pressure—and she let out a scream.

Alarmed, the German doctor returned to the hospital to examine the x-rays that had been taken there. Upon closer inspection, he found what the previous doctors had missed the fractures in her pubic bone and ischium, both parts of the lower pelvis. At least now we knew where the pain came from. I then consulted one of the most respected orthopedic surgeons in Manila to determine the best course of action. Since the bones were still well-aligned, he advised that surgical intervention wasn't necessary. Instead, Aline would need to remain on strict bed rest in order for the fractures to heal naturally.

And so, for the next six to eight weeks, Aline stayed confined to her bed, gradually recovering until she could walk again safely. The experience was not only physically painful but emotionally draining for her. In many ways, Manila had been a string of hardships, and this incident marked a turning point. She began longing deeply to return to Germany, where life was more familiar, stable, and safe.

In October 1995, I had the opportunity to become acquainted with projects in the *PACIFIC*. For a number of years, CBM had been supporting *Pacific*

Missionary Aviation (PMA), a flying medical service originally founded by the Liebenzeller Mission, an evangelical organization with a theological seminary located in the Black Forest town of Liebenzell. PMA was committed to serving patients in remote Pacific islands who were in need of medical care. Its primary catchment area included the Federated States of Micronesia (FSM), which consists of the islands of Yap, Chuuk, Pohnpei, and Kosrae, among others. These islands are separated by hundreds of miles of ocean. Apart from Micronesia, PMA also served the Republic of Palau and the U.S. territory of Guam, the largest of these Pacific islands.

To understand the vastness of the region and the small size of the islands, consider this: In terms of area, Micronesia is as large as the continental United States, but its population is only around 300,000 people, scattered across approximately 2,000 islands. And yet, the total land mass of these islands is less than half the size of Bali.

My first stop on my journey to the Pacific was the **REPUBLIC OF PALAU**. I visited a youth center and the island's hospital. There was no resident eye doctor on Palau and no eye clinic being held. Once a year, though, a team of American ophthalmologists would visit the hospital to screen patients and perform surgeries. At the time of my visit, a team of Japanese eye doctors had just arrived, and I had the chance to meet them. I also met with the Minister of Health at the hospital.

From Palau, PMA flew me to Pohnpei (or Ponape), the government seat of **MICRONESIA**. Here I met Edmund Kalau (1928–2014), the founder of PMA, who had spent more than 50 years in Micronesia, as well as his son and successor Norbert Kalau. In addition to its flying service, PMA ran a vocational training center on Pohnpei, a medical boat clinic called *Sea Haven*, a marine academy on Yap, a youth center on Palau, and an aviation service in the Philippines. At the Pohnpei hospital, I also met a doctor who had been trained in both ENT and eye surgery.

PMA flew to many of the smaller islands in Micronesia that no commercial airline would reach. Their fleet of eight single-engine aircraft included some that could carry up to four passengers, and others up to ten. The airstrips on these islands were narrow and relatively short, making only these light aircrafts capable of landing there safely.

In addition to Pohnpei, I visited the island of Yap, from where one of the pilots, Alex Tretnoff, took me on flights to two of the outer islands—Fais and Ulithi—each about an hour away from Yap. We flew in a Queenair Beechcraft 65-B80 (Image opposite page). To give you a sense of the scale: These islands are about as large as the airstrip itself (Image). Fais had around 200 inhabitants. There, we visited the local chief, whose wife had undergone cataract surgery on her right eye and was awaiting surgery for her left. Ulithi, with a population of about 100, was home to a surprisingly well-equipped high school with 200 students from different places. Many of the girls wore only traditional straw skirts, which was customary on this and other Pacific islands.

On our flight back to Yap, I was sitting next to the pilot and watched him operate his Beechcraft. I asked him—half in jest, half out of anxious curiosity: "What do I do if you have a heart attack and can no longer fly the plane?" He replied without missing a beat: "In that case, you should start praying."

I was also flown to **GUAM**, a U.S. territory considered the hub of the Pacific, where residents enjoyed all the conveniences of a modern American state. From Guam, I flew back to the Philippines.

In November 1995, I traveled once again to **INDONESIA** on what would be my last journey on behalf of CBM. I visited the Eyedrop Production Unit in Cikampek, east of Jakarta. We had arranged for a pharmacist from Sri Lanka to assist our partner organization in setting up the eye drop production, and I wanted to ensure that everything was ready before the expert's arrival. While there, I also met with an Indonesian ophthalmologist who was performing a commendable number of cataract surgeries.

From Cikampek, I flew to Malang in East Java to visit a community-based rehabilitation (CBR) program initiated by its current director, a Dutch priest who had spent 40 years in Indonesia. He had built one of the most impressive CBR programs I had seen anywhere. Begun as a single center for people with disabilities, this program had, under the leadership of Father Janssen, grown into a comprehensive community-based network serving some 2,000 individuals. During my visit, a CBR training course was underway for 24 future field workers, all of whom were fully engaged in practical, hands-on exercises.

I also visited a hospital in Singosari, just outside of Malang, where we had previously sponsored a doctor for training in India. In addition, I spent time at a Talking Book Library operated by a local foundation that served blind children. Since braille textbooks were largely unavailable, they were recording schoolbooks on tape for the blind students.

In the summer of 1996, my six-year overseas contract with CBM came to an end. While I could have imagined staying in the Philippines for another year or two, Aline was eager to return home to Germany. As CBM had not offered me a position at their German headquarters in Bensheim, I began exploring alternative opportunities. I was turning 50 in July of that year—an age that felt appropriate for a new chapter with a different employer.

On one of my final trips to Germany, I had reached out to a former colleague of mine, Günther Bitzer, who was now serving as Executive Director of World Vision Germany, headquartered in Friedrichsdorf. At the time I visited him, there was no position he could offer me. But a few months later, when his Public Relations Director resigned, Bitzer contacted me with an offer to take over that role and serve as World Vision's Press Spokesperson. Though I had little experience in public relations, I accepted the position, trusting that I would receive proper training if needed.

As we prepared to move from Manila back to Germany, I began phasing out of my responsibilities as Regional Director, and CBM started the search for a suitable replacement. Again, we had all our furniture and belongings packed into a shipping container. I'll never forget the care and precision of the Filipino packing team—how meticulously they wrapped and organized every item into small and large boxes. Along with the furniture we had acquired in Malaysia, we also had collected numerous antique pieces and decorative items: here in the Philippines, in China, and in India.

I officially ended my work in Manila at the end of June 1996, bidding farewell to my team and many friends we had made during our time there.

Reflecting on my years with CBM, I often felt that my work was aligned with the very heart of what Jesus of Nazareth had taught: to care for the blind and the deaf, for the sick and the disabled, for the marginalized and the outcast. I had seen firsthand how people with disabilities—especially in the developing world—were often hidden away by families who felt ashamed or embarrassed because of them. The concept of integration was still foreign to many, and few understood the possibilities for educating and empowering blind, deaf, or physically disabled individuals to become fully contributing members of society.

I came to see my work with CBM as part of building the "Kingdom of God"—that vision Jesus so often spoke of in his teachings and parables. It meant that every person, regardless of ability or disability, is treated with dignity and respect and is welcomed and integrated into society.

I also came to believe that all of us are, in some way, "disabled"—we all have our limitations and weaknesses, and we each compensate them by cultivating our strengths. I had witnessed people with disabilities achieve incredible things, and I believe every one of them deserves access to education and training that allows them to thrive and be respected for who they are and can become.

Upon our return to Germany, we knew it would take about six weeks for the container to arrive, and we set ourselves the goal of finding a house within that time. Since I was to begin work with World Vision in Friedrichsdorf on July 1, 1996, we looked for a home in the surrounding area. Eventually, we found a house in Friedberg that suited us perfectly. When the container arrived, we were able to move everything in.

The house had a lovely garden and a small fish pond. It was spacious and well laid out. Aline and I each had our own rooms, and there was a guest room for Patrick whenever he came to visit us from London, where he was studying physics and mathematics. I also had a room for our model train which I set up again. The basement included a small apartment that we rented out, several cellar rooms, and—rather unusual—a fully equipped fallout shelter. The previous owner, an American fearful of Russian nuclear potential, had installed it. I turned it into my painting studio.

I never intended to sell my art work, but the house was large enough to hang my paintings throughout. Our home was also filled with Asian antiques and artifacts, and visitors were often astonished and intrigued by the decor. Even the entrance to the basement was framed by a grand, custom-carved wooden door from Bali, painted in rich red and gold tones—a striking reminder of our life in Asia. At the time, I hoped we would spend the rest of our lives there—but unfortunately, that was not to be …

A Vision for the World

Working for World Vision was an entirely different experience compared to my time with the Christian Blind Mission. Unlike CBM, which focused primarily on serving the blind and disabled, World Vision was dedicated to alleviating general poverty and hunger across the developing world. Its mission involved working hand in hand with local communities in Africa, Asia, and Latin America to improve lives through education, healthcare, clean water and sanitation, agricultural initiatives, and economic development. In addition, World Vision was actively engaged in emergency relief efforts in response to natural disasters such as droughts, earthquakes, and floods; as well as in advocacy work and the promotion of justice and human rights.

A key difference between World Vision and CBM was structural: World Vision was not merely a funding agency. It directly implemented its own programs through national offices in more than 90 countries, employing nearly 100,000 staff worldwide.

One of its primary fundraising tools was the child sponsorship program. Donating sponsors were regularly updated on specific children they supported—though these children were part of broader Area Development Programs (ADPs) that benefited entire communities. These programs, designed in close cooperation with local stakeholders and in alignment with their expressed priorities, provided clean drinking water, basic medical care, education, and vocational and agricultural training.

My role, too, shifted significantly. Rather than being involved in overseas project work, I was tasked with improving World Vision's public image in Germany. At the time, the concept of child sponsorships still faced significant criticism from competing German NGOs. One of my key responsibilities was to reshape public perception and defend the sponsorship model. Over time, these efforts paid off. Today, child sponsorships are widely accepted in Germany, and World Vision Germany has become a respected and influential player in the country's non-governmental landscape.

In my position, I worked closely with the German media and also built strong networks with other development NGOs. I played a leading role in developing standards and ethical guidelines for organizational quality, transparency, and communication. I was also instrumental in drafting ethical codices for public messaging as well as for governance and accountability. In designing these codices, I also proposed the creation of a "board of arbitration" to address complaints or accusations of mismanagement by development NGOs—an initiative that was fully accepted, and I became its first chairperson.

A significant part of my work involved raising awareness on pressing global issues—among the general public, political decision-makers, and journalists. These issues included child malnutrition, street children, child labor, modern slavery, the use of child soldiers, sexual abuse, female genital mutilation, and the complex challenges posed by HIV and AIDS. Thankfully, I was able to employ a small team of co-workers who helped me carry out these public relation tasks. I often felt they were doing a better job than myself.

In the beginning, I felt an urgent need to master the craft of public relations. How does one, for instance, compose a compelling press release? Beyond consulting a special book on the subject, I reached out to the chief executive of the German branch of the Associated Press. He kindly referred me to one of his team members—Christian Liebig—a fine, intelligent young gentleman who graciously offered his support over a period of time.

142

A few years later, Christian—by then working for a weekly news magazine in Munich and now also engaged to a young woman from an aristocratic family—volunteered to report on the second Iraq war in 2003 as an "embedded journalist." When American forces advanced into Baghdad to depose Saddam Hussein, Christian made the seemingly cautious decision to remain at a safe distance rather than accompany the troops into Baghdad. Tragically, that precaution proved fatal. He lost his life in a missile strike on the outskirts of the capital city. As Christian Liebig had been a supporter of World Vision, his wife-to-be, his parents, and the magazine he had worked for, founded a small NGO to raise funds for poverty alleviation in Africa. They offered to closely co-operate with World Vision.

To deepen my understanding of public relations, I enrolled in two excellent training courses, which provided me with a solid foundation in the principles and practices of the field. Remarkably, just three weeks after I began my work, World Vision was prominently featured on Germany's most-watched newscast, the *Tagesthemen*.

I wrote numerous press releases and articles for a wide array of media outlets on diverse topics. I even launched a magazine specifically for journalists, ensuring they were regularly updated on key developments within World Vision. Over time, I gave many interviews to both radio and television journalists, particularly during periods of disaster relief. The longest of these interviews was a 40-minute live telecast with one of the major television channels (MDR), during which viewers could call in with questions of all kinds.

I was frequently asked to contribute articles to various magazines, covering a wide range of issues—from general poverty and development cooperation to specific topics such as poverty of women, the plight of child soldiers, or children living with HIV/AIDS. Gradually, I found myself becoming a journalist in my own right.

As Director of Public Relations, I also took responsibility for shaping World Vision Germany's mission statements. Early on, I asked a fundamental question: "What is World Vision's vision for the world?" To my surprise, no one had a clear answer. While a set of core values existed already, there was no official mission or vision statement available.

Determined to address that deficit, I encouraged my colleagues to engage in a collaborative process. An organizational vision cannot be handed down from above—it must emerge organically from within the organization. Together, we initiated that process, eventually producing a series of documents articulating our mission, purpose, and principles. And this is the Vision Statement we came up with:

"We have a vision of a just world, where all people live in dignity and lead meaningful lives; a world that refuses to tolerate hunger and deprivation and is driven by a spirit of reconciliation. A world where people nurture wholesome relationships—with themselves, with one another, with God, and with creation. A world in which nations respect each other and live in peace. – As Christians from various denominations, we seek to alleviate material, mental, and spiritual suffering through acts of love and compassion. We are united in our hope for a better future and our sense of responsibility for the well-being of humanity. Our special concern is for the children of this world."

It was only years later that World Vision International also articulated its own vision statement—simple in form, yet profound in meaning:

> *Our vision for every child, life in all its fullness.*
> *Our prayer for every heart, the will to make it so.*

In defining our working principles, we were guided by three overarching goals: *First*, to bring swift and compassionate humanitarian relief where urgently needed. *Second*, to support sustainable, long-term development. *Third*, to advocate boldly for justice and human rights through lobbying and public campaigns.

At the heart of all these efforts stood some non-negotiable priorities: We resolved (1) to put children first, (2) to ensure the empowerment of those we serve, and (3) to confront the *roots* of poverty—not merely its visible *symptoms*.

As vital as such guiding principles are for any organization, my primary mission as Director of Public Relations was to cultivate a solid, credible reputation for World Vision. Experience from the business world had already made one truth abundantly clear: a reputation built over years can be undone in a single day, by a single misstep. Rebuilding trust, once lost, is a far slower climb.

The media, in this delicate balance, plays a central role. Keeping journalists consistently informed—about who we are, what we do, and how we do it—is a task that demands patience and persistence. It may seem tedious at times, but it is essential. In the long run, transparency and steady communication are what allow trust to take root and grow.

Of course, no matter how strategic or thoughtful a public relations campaign may be, there are moments when events unfold that lie entirely beyond the control of any press office. One such moment came with stark clarity on Monday, June 29th, 2002.

That night, deep in the darkness of Southern Sudan, several World Vision staff members were abducted at gunpoint. In the course of the kidnapping, one Kenyan colleague was killed. The remaining three were forced to march barefoot for long, grueling hours through unfamiliar terrain.

There had been yet another Kenyan staff member, a woman, who—by sheer instinct and presence of mind—had managed to hide herself during the abduction chaos. She later informed World Vision of what had happened, offering the first fragile thread of hope in a moment of heartbreak and fear. One of the three abducted workers was a Kenyan, and the other two were Germans—one of whom, Ekki Forberg, I knew personally and held in high esteem.

For us at World Vision Germany, we wondered how to act. Although the temptation was there to go public, we first chose silence. Out of concern for the safety of our abducted colleagues, we refrained from informing the German public. We feared that any premature publicity might endanger delicate negotiations underway to secure their release. But that silence was short-lived. That very evening, a journalist from dpa, Germany's leading news agency, called me directly.

"Can you confirm the abduction?" he asked.

I confirmed it—nothing more. No details, no speculation. Only the truth that could not be hidden.

Meanwhile, far from the offices and headlines, the abducted three were enduring a brutal ordeal. None of them was accustomed to marching long distances, let alone barefoot under the unforgiving Sudanese sun. Fear stalked every step—fear of landmines, of venomous snakes, of scorpions hidden beneath the sand. They were given barely enough food or water to keep them healthy. On the day of their capture, the United Nations dispatched a plane to Sudan to make contact with the rebel faction responsible. Word reached us that a ransom had been demanded by the group's leader.

Within hours, the story exploded into the German press. The kidnapping dominated the news cycle. Our phones rang endlessly. Journalists called for answers, for updates, for human stories—and yet, we had so little to offer. Silence had given way to a vacuum, and still, we knew only fragments. Then, a glimmer of hope.

After several anxious days, we learned that one of the two German hostages had been released—freed, unexpectedly, by a rival rebel group. There was relief, yes—but it was tempered by the haunting knowledge that two of our people still remained in captivity, one a Kenyan, the other my good friend Ekki.

And then, finally, on Saturday morning—August 3rd, five days after the abduction—came the news we had longed for: the remaining two hostages had also been released. To our great surprise, no ransom appeared to have been paid. The International Red Cross sent a plane to retrieve them from Sudan, and the next day, I was able to speak with Ekki by phone. His voice was weary but clear. He and his fellow German colleague had decided to return home without delay.

On Tuesday, August 6th, they arrived at Frankfurt Airport. I had already reserved a room for a press conference, knowing the media would be waiting. One of the two Germans limped visibly, his body still bearing the marks of that punishing journey. Ekki, unable to walk at all, was wheeled into the room. I welcomed them both and greeted the many journalists who had gathered. I then invited our director, Günther Bitzer, to say a few words of welcome, after which I turned to Ekki and his companion and asked whether they felt ready to share their story.

They did. With quiet dignity, they recounted what had happened. There were no theatrics—only the raw, understated power of two men who had endured the ordeal, had survived, and now stood, or sat, before the world once more. They willingly answered every question, their relief at being home etched into every word, every pause between sentences.

The press conference was widely covered. Two national TV channels broadcasted it in its entirety, live—bearing witness not just to a story of survival, but to the enduring strength of the human spirit.

Though my role as World Vision Germany's Director of Public Relations and Press Spokesman no longer required me to travel abroad to oversee projects, there were still occasions when special trips became necessary. One such occasion came soon after I had begun my work in July of 1996.

A journalist by the name of Markus Mallmann was planning a feature article for a magazine specializing in development cooperation. It was agreed that I would accompany him to *ETHIOPIA* to provide insight into one of World Vision's projects. And so, in September 1996, we set off—bound for Addis Ababa, and from there, journeyed by car some 360 kilometers north to Antsokia Valley, a place once synonymous with hunger and suffering.

Only a decade earlier, Antsokia had been the epicenter of one of the most devastating famines the world had witnessed. It had given rise to the "Live Aid" concerts organized by Bob Geldof in 1985 which were held, among other places, at the Wembley Stadium in London and at the John F. Kennedy Stadium in Philadelphia. Live Aid put poverty in Africa on the world's agenda like nothing before had ever done. World Vision, among other humanitarian agencies, had provided emergency relief during that time—but the organization came to see that sacks of grain alone could not heal a land so deeply wounded. To offer food in a time of crisis was necessary—but to stop there would have been to abandon the people once the headlines faded.

146

Instead, World Vision resolved to walk a longer path. They launched a bold, integrated development program—one that would address not just hunger, but the causes of hunger. The focus turned to sustainable agriculture and reforestation, to education and healthcare, to clean water and infrastructure. Roads were carved into the landscape so that goods could reach markets. A local administration was put in place, not only to oversee the work, but to give the people the power to shape their own future.

At every turn, the question was asked: *What do you need? What do you value?* The people of Antsokia were not treated as passive recipients, but as co-authors of their own vision and mission. The pace of progress was determined by the community itself—by its will, its labor, its dreams.

When we arrived, what we saw was nothing short of remarkable. The once-barren hills now bore witness to life. Rows upon rows of trees had taken root. "Trees are a good defense against hunger," we were told. They summon rain from the sky, hold the soil in place, retain water in the ground, and in time, offer timber and income. In a single year, 1.3 million seedlings had been planted.

But forestry was only part of the story. Agriculture had also been reborn. Where once only corn, millet, and teff were grown—the latter used to make the soft, spongy *injera* that is a staple of Ethiopian cuisine—now there were avocados, papayas, citrus fruits, mangos, apples. There were also coffee beans, peas, and legumes. The soil had been asked to give more, and it had responded.

And then we asked the question that loomed, quietly, behind every success: *What will happen when World Vision leaves? Will progress last?* The program director did not hesitate to respond.

"We have changed the thinking and expectations of the people here," he said. "They have embraced new ways of farming, new dietary habits, new understandings of hygiene. They see the forest as something to protect, not plunder. And they no longer wish for their children to grow up without school or skills."

The project, once born of desperation, had become a beacon. A showpiece of what development could mean—not merely the absence of hunger, but the presence of dignity. An entire region, once left to the mercy of drought and despair, was now writing a new story—with its own hands.

With these impressions still vivid in our minds, Markus Mallmann and I made our way back to Addis Ababa. My camera was heavy with captured moments—faces, places, fragments of change. When we passed a group of Ethiopian soldiers standing by the roadside, I instinctively took a photograph. But just a hundred meters on, more soldiers flagged us down. One approached us and told me calmly, yet firmly, that photographing the army was forbidden. He asked me to remove the film from my camera and hand it over.

I explained that the roll contained important images—memories we needed to take home. But he insisted. I refused. Instead, we began speaking openly with them—explaining our purpose, asking about the security situation. The tension lingered. They repeated their demand several times, warning they would take the camera if I didn't comply. Still, I held my ground, silent and unwavering, waiting for the moment to pass. And in the end, it did. They let us go. We returned home, Markus wrote a fine article, and I went back to my usual day-to-day business.

On another journey, I set my sights on the **BALKANS**, where the Kosovo War was raging—a bitter and complex conflict that unfolded between February 1998 and June 1999. It pitted the Serbian regime, desperate to maintain control over the province, against the Kosovo Liberation Army, a separatist militia fighting for Kosovo's independence. But beneath the political banners lay deeper wounds: ethnic fault lines and historical grievances, as most Kosovars were ethnic Albanians, while the Yugoslav forces were largely Serbian.

By March 1999, the violence had escalated into a brutal campaign of expulsion. In a matter of weeks, more than half a million Kosovars were forced to flee—375,000 to Albania, and another 150,000 to Montenegro. As they crossed the borders, they were often stripped of their passports, their possessions, and their very sense of belonging.

I wanted to see the situation with my own eyes—to witness the plight of the displaced and to understand how World Vision was responding to this humanitarian catastrophe. On May 1st, 1999, I set out in a World Vision vehicle and drove southward through Italy, pausing only once in the ancient Republic of **SAN MARINO**, before driving on to Southern Italy.

From the port city of Bari, I took a ferry across the Adriatic to **ALBANIA**. There, at the coastal town of Durres, fate introduced me to a young Kosovar named Gazmend Cikaci who spoke excellent German and who gave me directions for my onward travel. I saw him again in Prizren on another trip and would not hear from him again for some 25 years, until a WhatsApp message arrived out of the blue, for reasons that I will explain later.

I drove on to Tirana, Albania's capital, and joined World Vision's local staff. Together, we travelled south to Fier, where World Vision was housing around 1,000 refugees in a former tobacco factory. In the nearby town of Vlore, there were already over 10,000 refugees, with the numbers swelling by the hour. I witnessed the distribution of food and essential supplies. Smaller NGOs turned to World Vision to take the lead—to coordinate, to stabilize, to respond to the chaos with structure and care.

In Vlore, I met a young Kosovar couple who had lost their home, but managed to rescue a portion of their savings. The woman was a well-known singer in Kosovo, her voice silenced by war but her spirit unbroken.

148

Back in Tirana, I saw yet more displaced families—some crammed into metal containers, trying to rebuild a semblance of life. One man told me how Serbian forces had burned his house, looted his belongings, and taken everything of value. Another claimed to have witnessed the execution of 30 of his fellow Kosovars. The stories were heavy, the air thick with grief and disbelief.

From Tirana, I traveled to Morina near Kosovo, the border town, where thousands streamed in—exhausted, disoriented, with little more than the clothes on their backs. I saw an old woman being carried across the border, her face blank with fatigue, and a young mother pushing her newborn child in a wheelbarrow, both fragile and defiant in the face of devastation. Many refugees had been on the move for weeks, always watching for danger, always uncertain of what lay ahead. What they had lost was not just homes and possessions, but entire lifetimes of effort and memory. Their desperation was palpable.

From there I drove north to **MONTENEGRO**, where I met with World Vision staff in Podgorica and visited a warehouse stocked with aid supplies. I also accompanied a team on a truck to Rozaje, near the border to Kosovo, where we delivered food and other necessities to the newly arrived. From there, I drove back to Podgorica and continued on to **BOSNIA-HERZE-GOVINA** with its capital Sarajevo, where the scars of war were still raw—Bosnian neighborhoods reduced to rubble by Serbian forces in years past.

On Friday, May 14th, I began the long return journey home—northward through Croatia, Slovenia, and Austria. By nightfall, after covering 1,500 kilometers in a single day, I was back in Germany, carrying with me stories I could never forget, and a heart made heavier—and strangely fuller—by all I had seen.

A couple of months later, the tide began to turn. International pressure mounted, and NATO's controversial yet resolute bombing campaign—undertaken on humanitarian grounds—forced the hand of Belgrade. The war drew to a close with the signing of the Kumanovo Agreement on June 9th, 1999. The Serbs agreed to withdraw from Kosovo, and a fragile sense of hope returned to a battered land.

With the first rays of postwar dawn breaking over the Balkans, thousands of Kosovar refugees began their journey home—returning not to safety or comfort, but to ruins. I flew once more to the region, eager to understand the new reality unfolding in the wake of devastation. Landing in Pristina, I made my way to Prizren, where I visited Gazmend Cikaci, the young man I had first encountered weeks earlier on the ferry to Albania. There was something quietly powerful about that reunion—a thread of human continuity amid the chaos.

By mid-June, some 400,000 refugees had crossed back from Albania, Macedonia, and Montenegro into Kosovo. They returned to shattered homes, scorched villages, and fields haunted by the cruel legacy of land mines. In Prizren, World Vision was doing what it could to help—providing shelter for families left without roofs, walls, or even doors to close behind them. But the ground was not safe. Mines, cruelly and indiscriminately planted, lay hidden beneath the soil, waiting. I met survivors of these hidden dangers—one man who had lost both eyes to an explosion. His gaze, though sightless, still held pain and resolve.

In the village of Petrova, near Shtimle, I stood at the edge of a tragedy. Twenty young men had been separated from their families just before NATO forces entered the area. They were beaten, their ribs shattered beneath boots and rifle butts, and finally knifed or shot, their bodies tossed into hurried graves. I saw the burial sites myself—quiet mounds of earth, each one a testimony to a life ended in cruelty.

The tragedy of Kosovo was part of a much broader unraveling—the aftermath of communism's collapse. When the Soviet Union disintegrated, new nations emerged from its former shell—Ukraine, Belarus, Georgia, Moldova and others. But the ripple effect reached into the Balkans as well. Yugoslavia, a federation of diverse ethnicities held together more by will than unity, also began to disintegrate. Though it had never been a Soviet satellite, its cohesion had depended on one man: Josip Tito.Under his iron grip, the country had remained one—through suppression, not harmony. But when he died, the once-unified Yugoslavia fractured into its constituent parts: Slovenia, Croatia, (North) Macedonia, Montenegro, Kosovo, Bosnia-Herzegovina—as well as Serbia, the largest and most dominant of them all.

Eventually, most of the breakaway republics emerged as independent states. Kosovo, too, declared its independence unilaterally in February 2008. Though its sovereignty has been recognized by over 100 nations, Serbia continues to withhold acknowledgment, and tensions still simmer beneath the surface.

The Yugoslav and Kosovo Wars offer us a hard-earned lesson: A multiethnic state can only endure through freedom, not fear—through democratic inclusion, not authoritarian control. True stability arises not from suppression, but from giving space to each identity to breathe, speak, and self-govern. Suppressing national identities may buy temporary calm, but it always carries within it the seed of backlash—nationalist, fascist, and xenophobic. When people are denied their voice, they eventually scream. The Balkans screamed in the 1990s. May we learn to listen before others must do the same.

Later that year, in August 1999, I embarked on my first and only trip to **LATIN AMERICA**, a journey that would open my eyes to the world of advocacy and the wider struggles faced by the marginalized. World Vision organized an Advocacy Conference, and I flew first to Rio de Janeiro, before making my way to Recife, where the workshop took place.

It was here, amidst the passionate discussions and fervent debates, that I came to a sobering realization: For an international NGO like World Vision, it was not enough to merely run or support development programs. Our work had to extend beyond the provision of aid—it had to include a steadfast commitment to advocating for human rights and social justice. We had to speak for those whose voices have been silenced, and challenge the systems that perpetuate inequality.

One of the prominent advocacy themes at the time was the plight of impoverished nations burdened by insurmountable debt. The "Jubilee 2000" campaign had gained momentum, calling on Western creditor nations to forgive the crushing debts of poor countries. The rationale was clear: These nations were trapped in a cycle of repayments, where debt and interest only served to line the pockets of the wealthy nations, leaving the poor to sink deeper into poverty. The call for debt relief was not just an economic demand; it was a plea for justice and mercy—and a demand for a more equitable global system.

But the struggles of the world's poor were not confined to financial burdens alone. At the conference, we also discussed a myriad of other critical advocacy issues: gender inequality, the global health crisis, the devastating impact of HIV and AIDS, the dire need for improved maternal and child healthcare, and the urgent call for stronger child protection measures. Each of these issues, though varied in their scope, shared a common thread—a relentless demand for dignity and rights for all people, regardless of their birthplace or their social status.

As I listened to the stories, the statistics, and the impassioned pleas for action, I was reminded of the profound responsibility we carried as advocates of the poor. Our work was not just about providing relief—it was about fighting for a world in which justice prevails, where the most vulnerable are not forgotten, and where humanity stands united in its resolve to create lasting change.

In the year 2000, the World EXPO took place in Hanover, Germany, and World Vision Germany participated alongside other NGOs in managing one of the most distinctive pavilions at the event. Our pavilion, built in the shape of a whale (Image next page), quickly became a centerpiece of the EXPO, standing out not just for its unique architecture, but for its powerful message. Inside the "Whale," as it was affectionately called, was a communication center designed to inform and inspire visitors about global issues and the work being done to address them.

As the Public Relations Director, I was partly responsible for coordinating World Vision's activities within the pavilion. Our goal was simple yet ambitious: to reach as many people as possible and inform them about the work World Vision was doing in developing countries. Among the many topics we presented to the EXPO visitors were some of the most pressing issues of the time: humanitarian relief, integrated development programs, child sponsorships, assistance for slum inhabitants, the plight of child soldiers, the

practice of female genital mutilation, and the dark reality of bonded labor—modern slavery. We also highlighted the importance of debt relief for poor countries, focusing on the "Year of Jubilee" campaign. We shed light on war-traumatized children, child-led households in East Africa due to high HIV/ AIDS death rates, street children, children living in rubbish dumps, and the so-called "tunnel children" of Ulan Bator, Mongolia.

The direct interaction with EXPO visitors was invaluable, as it allowed us to bring the stories of real people into their lives, making the abstract tangible. We invited numerous individuals to speak about their work and experiences.

Among those who spoke at the pavilion were Aaron Ward, a clown who brought laughter to war-traumatized children in Kosovo, Bosnia, and Montenegro; Grace Acayo, a former child soldier from Uganda; Evelyn, a World Vision co-worker who

worked to rehabilitate former child soldiers (Image: Kurt with Grace and Evelyn); and Hamil Hamzaj, a refugee from Kosovo. We also heard from Remzi Osmani, a Kosovar folklore singer, Lisbeth Speelmann, a World Vision psychologist working in Kosovo, and from Safia Hussein, a victim of female genital mutilation (FGM). Each of these speakers brought a unique and powerful perspective to the subjects presented.

Another unforgettable moment at the EXPO 2000 was the performance of the World Vision choir called "Youth Ambassadors." This choir, composed of 50 young people from 50 different countries, aged 14 to 18, traveled the world singing songs of peace, reconciliation, disaster relief, and poverty alleviation. Their performances were met with rapturous applause, a beautiful example of how young people from all corners of the globe—diverse in culture, ethnicity, and skin color—could come together in harmony to advocate for a better, more just world. The choir became a symbol of hope, unity, and the power of youth to make a difference. Their message was simple yet profound: despite our differences, we are all part of the same human family, and it is our collective responsibility to care for one another.

In the end, the EXPO 2000 in Hanover was a special and transformative experience for World Vision. It gave us the opportunity to present our work and concerns to a vast and diverse public, many of whom may never have encountered World Vision's efforts otherwise. It was a chance to showcase the breadth and depth of our programs, share the stories of those whose lives had been touched by our work, and most importantly, inspire others to join us in our mission to bring about lasting change. Nearly one million people visited our pavilion and learned about World Vision.

In January 2000, UN negotiations were held in Geneva concerning the use of children as soldiers, preceded by a conference of non-governmental organizations (NGOs) on the same topic. The goal was to secure the approval of a UN "Optional Protocol" that would prohibit the use of child soldiers and raise the minimum age for military recruitment. The NGOs also planned international conferences to engage policymakers on this critical issue.

My next journey was directly related to this cause. It was my first visit to **UGANDA**. Philipp Hahn, a journalist from one of Germany's major private TV channels (ProSieben), approached me with a request to help him produce three documentaries about child soldiers. I agreed, and in 2001, the journalist, his cameraman, and I traveled to Gulu in northern Uganda. There, World Vision was running a rehabilitation center for children and young people who had been abducted and forced to serve as soldiers in the "Lord's Resistance Army" (LRA), a rebel group led by Joseph Kony.

Kony, a member of the northern Acholi tribe, believed that the Ugandan government had unfairly repressed his people. He founded the LRA, claiming to be guided by divine revelation and to be in constant communion with Christ. His original goal was to fight the Ugandan army, but over time, he turned against his own people, believing them to be collaborators with the government. Kony's forces abducted thousands of children, primarily from the Acholi community, and forcibly trained them to become soldiers.

Many of these children were severely manipulated and brutalized. Kony knew that children, unlike adults, could be more easily controlled and coerced into committing atrocities. The children were taught to kill using clubs, machetes, or—when available—Kalashnikov rifles, which were quite easy for them to handle. Even children as young as 10 years were often given AK-47s and taught to kill with ruthless efficiency.

During attacks on villages, the LRA would set fire to straw huts at night to lure the inhabitants outside, where they would be slaughtered by the child soldiers. These young fighters would line up and shoot on command, advancing through the village, killing virtually everything alive. The level of violence these children were forced to commit hardened many of them, desensitizing them to the horrors of war and atrocity. I met a group of former child soldiers who were now 17 or 18 years old, and I couldn't help but think to myself, "I wouldn't want to meet any of them in the dark."

Despite the horrors, some children managed to escape, though many were deeply traumatized. To help them recover, World Vision supported a rehabilitation center in Gulu where these young survivors could begin to heal. At the center, they learned that the acts they had been forced to commit were not normal, and they were encouraged to confront the reality of their actions. The program provided a space for these children to share their stories, express their feelings, and understand the profound impact of what they had done.

One of the most challenging aspects of this rehabilitation process was to reintegrate the children into their families. Many of the children had been away for years, and their families were often hesitant or fearful to welcome them back. Yet, through the support of World Vision and other organizations, these young people slowly began to rebuild their lives, learning to live peacefully and trying to undo the trauma they had endured during their time in the LRA.

One of the girls who had been abducted by the LRA and forced to kill was Christine. By the time I spoke to her, she was 17 years old. Christine had been kidnapped when she was just 12, along with her father and brother. The three of them were made to carry heavy loads for many miles. Her father, burdened with 50 kilograms, eventually collapsed under the weight. He was beaten nearly to death and left behind. He survived, but was disabled for the rest of his life. Christine herself was forced to march for seven days, carrying

20 liters of oil and 5 kilograms of salt on her back—virtually without rest and with hardly any sleep. The little food they were given was eaten while walking, and every two days, they were provided with only a quarter liter of water.

Christine stayed with the Lord's Resistance Army (LRA) for two years. There were times when they had no water, and occasionally she was forced to drink her own urine. Joseph Kony, the leader of the LRA, told the girls that they would be given as wives to commanders. If they refused, they would be killed. Christine witnessed another girl who refused to become a commander's wife, and she was instantly executed. Christine herself became the eighth wife of one of the commanders, a man named Vincent, who raped her and often beat her.

Being trained as a soldier in the LRA was grueling. Some children did not survive the training. Christine's brother died during it. On one occasion, Kony told about 1,000 children that they had five minutes to put on their uniforms, assemble, and be ready with their weapons and ammunition. If they failed to do so, they would be killed. As Kony had promised, he executed about 30 children who did not make it in time.

Many of the children often thought about escaping. Some succeeded, but many did not. Christine shared the story of five girls who tried to flee but were caught. Two of them were killed in front of everyone as a warning to others. Christine also contemplated escape, but the chances were slim.

One day, Vincent, her commander and "husband," took a group of child soldiers on a raid in Northern Uganda. It turned out that the area was familiar to Christine. Fearing for her safety during the raid, Vincent left her behind, not wanting her to be killed, as she was very pretty. He ordered three soldiers to keep an eye on her to ensure she didn't run away. But Christine knew this was her only chance. As the soldiers were distracted, she shot the one closest to her and bolted. The other two soldiers tried to shoot her with their Kalashnikov rifles, and one bullet actually grazed her head. But Christine didn't stop running.

When she reached a safe distance, she revealed herself to local villagers, who helped her reach a hospital, where her head injury was treated. The hospital staff also discovered she was four months pregnant. After receiving care, she was sent to the Gulu World Vision center for former child soldiers, where she received both material and psychological support. It was at this center that she encountered one of the boys who had tried to shoot her. He was stunned to see her alive. "We fired so many shots at you, we were sure you were dead," he told her.

At the time I spoke with Christine, she was still grappling with the weight of the killings she had been forced to commit. She reassured herself that she had acted under duress, compelled at gunpoint. Often, it was a matter of killing or being killed. On one occasion, Christine and 29 other young soldiers were sent into combat against another rebel group. Only five of them made it back alive. The child soldiers were routinely sent to attack villages, burn homes, and kill everyone over the age of 30. The younger children were taken and trained to be soldiers. With her machine gun, Christine was forced to kill many civilians. Had she refused, she would have been killed herself.

When Christine gave birth to her baby, she became deeply desperate. She was still a child herself and felt completely unprepared to care for a newborn. Fortunately, a World Vision donor stepped in and funded her education. It was at this school, where she was trying to rebuild her life, that I met Christine and learned her story.

Another former child soldier I came to know well was Grace Acayo. She had been invited to speak at the United Nations Conference "Women 2000" in New York, where she shared her experience with the Lord's Resistance Army (LRA). Kidnapped at age 15, she was forced to kill for the LRA and given as the eleventh "wife" to a senior commander. After three years, she managed to escape during a gunfight between the LRA and the Ugandan Army. Ugandan soldiers brought her to the World Vision center in Gulu, where she received medical care and psychological support.

At the conference in New York, Grace appealed to the world to take stronger action against the use of children as soldiers. On her way back to Uganda, we invited her to stop by at the World Vision pavilion at the EXPO 2000 in Hanover, which she gladly did. She told us what had hurt most was being separated from her siblings, who had also been abducted. She rarely saw her nine-year-old sister, and her older brother remained missing.

At the EXPO, Grace encountered a world unlike anything she had known—one of light, peace, and wonder. Instead of fear and poverty, she was surrounded by modern marvels and international figures. She was especially struck by Queen Silvia of Sweden who visited the EXPO, not for her title but for her humility. "I always thought a queen would wear a long, lavish dress," she confided to us with a smile. She also met the First Lady of Germany, the wife of then-President Rau.

After the EXPO, I met Grace again in Uganda and was glad to see she was doing well. Her visit to the West, and the kindness of those she met there, had inspired her. She had made up her mind to live a meaningful life—helping others even more in need than herself.

The use of child soldiers was still an urgent global issue at that time. Though children are defined as any person under 18, international law still allowed military recruitment from age 15 onward. In many African countries, where birth dates are often unknown, children as young as 12 or 13 were forced to become soldiers, even by the official armies. According to the United Nations, around 300,000 child soldiers were active worldwide by the year 2000. In Northern Uganda, the LRA alone was estimated to have abducted some 25,000 children. Most families in the region were affected. World Vision's center in Gulu helped rehabilitate about 7,000 former child soldiers.

In early 2002, the Ugandan Army deployed 10,000 troops into Southern Sudan in an attempt to capture Joseph Kony—but without success. He has never been caught, for all I know.

World Vision and other NGOs urged global leaders to outlaw the use of child soldiers entirely, calling for a minimum recruitment age of 18 worldwide. In 1998, several NGOs—including World Vision—formed the "Coalition to Stop the Use of Child Soldiers" (now known as Child Soldiers International). The Coalition organized the European Conference on the Use of Children as Soldiers, held in Berlin in October 1999. I helped organize the event and authored its final report. The conference drew policymakers from across Europe, including German Secretary of State Joschka Fischer. It concluded with a formal declaration urging European governments to end all military recruitment under the age of 18.

The Coalition organized similar conferences on other continents and worked to influence the UN Security Council to support the "Optional Protocol" against the use of children in Armed Conflict" (OPAC). The protocol was adopted by the UN in 2000 and entered into force in 2002. I had the opportunity to visit the then-President of the UN Security Council in New York myself, urging him to advocate for the protocol's broad adoption, which he promised to do.

My trip to Uganda, accompanied by Philipp Hahn, the German journalist, and his cameraman, resulted in three short films. These documented the lives of children once forced to fight for the LRA, and the work of World Vision in helping them return to their families and rebuild their lives.

In March 2001, I was asked to participate in a Communication Conference hosted by World Vision International in *MELBOURNE, AUSTRALIA*. One of the reasons for this meeting was a new campaign called "Global Movement for Children" for which UNICEF had solicited the support of World Vision, Save the Children and Plan International. The Movement was to culminate in a "Special Session on Children," held in September of that year by the UN General Assembly in New York. As part of that movement, World Vision was launching its own campaign called "Imagine a world where children are safe," which placed emphasis on the safety of children from child abuse, sexual exploitation, armed conflict, and violence at home. Another World Vision campaign was to raise awareness in the southern African nations regarding HIV/AIDS and how to prevent it.

This journey was my second visit to Australia, albeit limited to this southernmost city. On my way back home, I made a stopover in Bali where I met Aline who was coming from Germany, and we spent a couple of weeks vacationing on this beautiful island.

Another memorable journey took me to **KENYA**. One day, in 2001, a German film team reached out to World Vision for our support. They had just completed filming "Nowhere in Africa," shot about 300 kilometers north of Nairobi in a rural area called Mukutani. The film told the true story of a German-Jewish family that fled to Kenya in 1938 to escape persecution in Nazi Germany, and shows how the family struggled to get adjusted to the new African environment. Things were complicated because of the Second World War that soon began.

To create an authentic African setting, the film crew spent weeks filming in this remote region and even constructed a dirt road to Mukutani to transport equipment and personnel. The local community had offered their warm cooperation, and in return, benefited in small but meaningful ways from the production.

When filming wrapped, the team asked the villagers if there was anything they could do for them in gratitude for their hospitality. The elders gathered and made a simple, heartfelt request: extend the newly-built dirt road by another ten kilometers—to reach a market town where they could sell their produce and buy essential goods.

The film team, willing to help, turned to World Vision Germany to ask whether we could assist in building the extension of the road. They would provide the funding. I contacted our office in Nairobi and also visited the film's producer, Peter Herrmann, and its director, Caroline Link, both based in Munich. Later, I also met Juliane Köhler, who played the lead role in the movie. By then, it was 2002—the film had been completed, and I was invited to its premiere. And above all: it had just been nominated for an Academy Award for Best International Feature Film.

Peter Herrmann invited me to accompany him on a return trip to Kenya. He wanted to present the finished film to the people of Mukutani, who were eager to see what had come of the weeks of filming in their village. We flew to Nairobi and then continued on to Mukutani. There, we met some of the local actors and were warmly welcomed by the community. Peter screened the film for them. While most villagers did not speak English and couldn't follow the full story, they delighted in spotting familiar faces and places on screen.

We spoke with local elders about the road project. I explained that World Vision's Nairobi team would soon visit them to discuss the next steps. Later, the Nairobi office followed up to assess whether the road was truly the community's most urgent need. What about a school or a health clinic? "Those would be good," the elders said, "but the road is more urgent. We need a way to earn money, to sell our crops and buy what we lack."

And so, the road was built—funded by the film team and other donors, with World Vision managing the project. But our involvement didn't end there. We remained in Mukutani, supporting the community in other ways, long after the road was complete.

Not long afterward, "Nowhere in Africa" was awarded the Oscar for Best Foreign Film. I was thrilled—so was of course Caroline Link, who as the director of the motion picture received the Academy Award with grace and pride in Hollywood. Some time later, World Vision hosted a special dinner for the film crew. Caroline, who happens to be from Bad Nauheim—the very town where I now live—brought her golden Oscar with her (Image: Kurt with film director Caroline Link, CEO Gunther Bitzer, producer Peter Herrmann and chief actress Juliane Köhler).

My next journey took me once again to Africa. It was June 2003, and the purpose of the trip was to gain a fresh perspective on World Vision's integrated regional development work. I had first seen such a program in Ethiopia in 1996 (see above), not long after I had began working for World Vision. This time, my destination was *MALAWI* and *ZIMBABWE*. I first

flew to Johannesburg, then onward to Blantyre in Malawi—a country of some 12 million people at the time. World Vision Malawi operated 23 Area Development Programs (ADPs) across the country; and World Vision Germany supported five of them. The population within each ADP ranged from 20,000 to 100,000 people.

Together with local World Vision colleagues, we visited the Mphuka ADP, named after the local leader, Senior Chief Mphuka. One of the project's key pillars was agricultural development. Education was also a priority—but was rated second place, as children cannot learn well if they go hungry, or if they can't even make it to school because they are too weak.

159

The achievements here may have seemed modest at first glance, but for the people living there, they were milestones. One such initiative was the introduction of "intercropping"—the practice of planting different crops on the same land at different times of the year. This diversification led to greater food security. Some families had even been able to build better homes, acquire a television set, or dig fish ponds. Others invested in livestock breeding.

In education, the most pressing issue was the severe shortage of qualified teachers willing to live and work in remote rural areas—especially given the lack of proper housing. The student-teacher ratio stood at 238 to 1. Within the ADP, there were 15 primary schools serving 11,450 pupils, up from fewer than 10,000 in 1999. Common reasons for school dropouts included early pregnancies and the deaths of parents due to HIV/AIDS. We visited one of the schools ourselves, and the barely passable "road" leading to it made it painfully clear how much the infrastructure still needed improvement.

We then visited the Mpanda ADP, it became clear that the local community had embraced full ownership of the project. This ADP had 16 World Vision staff. Agricultural activity here focused on drought-resistant crops like cassava, sweet potatoes, and chickpeas. Some fields were irrigated using a relatively modern sprinkler system powered by a diesel generator.

The major health challenge, as elsewhere in Malawi, was HIV/AIDS. 16 percent of World Vision-sponsored children in the area were orphans and left to care for their own siblings. I met Christina, an 18-year-old girl looking after her 16-year-old sister and three brothers, aged 20, 10, and 9. For children like them, the daily question was stark: Should they go to school, or work the fields to keep the family fed?

The following day, I flew to Zimbabwe, where I visited the World Vision office in Harare and two Area Development Projects (ADPs) in the northeast of the country. Zimbabwe—formerly Rhodesia—was in the grip of political and economic turmoil. Longtime president Robert Mugabe (1987–2017) clung desperately to power, at the expense of the country's stability. A devastating famine in 2002 had left millions dependent on food aid. Mugabe's so-called "land reform," which stripped white farmers of their land and handed it to black owners without sufficient training or resources, had crippled agricultural productivity. Meanwhile, hyperinflation was eroding the already fragile purchasing power of ordinary citizens.

Our goal was to visit two ADPs. Patrick Nhuvira, the project manager for both, drove us 180 kilometers northeast to Chihoko. This ADP had been running for ten years and was nearing completion. It covered an area of some 1,200 square kilometers and served roughly 85,000 people. When I asked the board members how they would rate the change in their lives since the project began—on a scale of 1 to 100—they answered: "Ten years ago, it was about 40. Now it's around 80." There was still room for progress, but the difference was undeniable.

One improvement they mentioned was sanitation. Previously, people had used the "Bush System"—relieving themselves in the open, in the bush. Now, many had adopted the "Blair System," a simple squat toilet design introduced by a British-born Zimbabwean named Blair, vastly improving hygiene in the region. World Vision had helped build 500 such toilets in the area.

Clean water access had also transformed daily life. In the past, water came from rivers or stagnant pools. Now, it flowed from 168 drilled wells. Of course, wells rely on pumps, and pumps occasionally break. World Vision trained 50 local mechanics and equipped them with toolkits and spare parts to maintain the pumps.

Malaria was a major health threat, particularly to children. In response, mosquito nets and repellents had been widely distributed. HIV and AIDS remained another silent scourge—awareness was still limited, and preventive campaigns had yet to reach full scale.

In agriculture, 2,600 farmers received "loans" in the form of seeds and fertilizer. Upon repaying the loan—typically through part of their harvest— they became eligible for renewed support. Corn and cotton were the most requested crops, but diversification was increasing. Farmers began cultivating soya beans and peanuts, while others turned to livestock and milk production.

The second ADP we visited was in Mukumbura, near the Mozambican border. As this project had only recently started, there was little to observe in terms of progress. But we met Peter Pichler, an Austrian newly appointed to oversee the initiative. His first priority: repairing broken water pumps and training locals to maintain them.

When then travelled to Bulawayo in the south of Zimbabwe, where we observed a large-scale food distribution led by the World Food Program in collaboration with USAID and three NGOs—World Vision, CARE, and Catholic Relief Services. Some 1.3 million people were receiving food aid. We visited one of the distribution sites and a warehouse where tons of food and cooking oil were being stored and loaded onto trucks.

At the end of this intense journey, I had the chance to visit the famous Victoria Falls. Straddling the border between Zimbabwe and Zambia, the falls are over 5,000 feet wide and 350 feet high—forming the largest continuous sheet of falling water on Earth. Here, the Zambezi River plunges dramatically into a gorge below, creating a thunderous spectacle.

What makes Victoria Falls so remarkable is how close one can get to the action. On the Zimbabwean side, a footpath leads you almost into the mist itself. Unlike Niagara Falls, which must be viewed from a far distance, here you feel immersed—wrapped in spray, sound, and motion. I got so close to the falls that the mist nearly ruined my video camera. Still, the experience was unforgettable—a moment of natural awe that made up for the strain and fatigue of travel.

Apart from such project visits, I also attended numerous conferences and workshops covering a wide range of topics. These trips took me to cities such as London, Dublin, Paris, Brussels, Geneva, Vienna, New York, Seattle, Washington D.C., Toronto, and others.

In June 2004, I made yet another journey to **ADDIS ABABA** to take part in another World Vision advocacy workshop. One advocacy issue I was very much committed to was the Tobin Tax—named after James Tobin, the American economist who had proposed taxing short-term financial transactions. French activists took up this idea and founded *attac*, the "Association for the Taxation of Financial Transactions and for Citizens' Action."

Every day, bankers and financial managers move billions—sometimes trillions—of dollars and euros across global markets. These rapid-fire transactions often serve no purpose beyond generating short-term profits, while exerting a destabilizing influence on economies and societies. It was, in many ways, a symptom of unchecked neoliberal globalization—driven and accelerated by emerging computer technologies in the mid-1990s.

Tobin's idea was simple: a small tax on these high-frequency trades could hamper the massive transactions and also generate enormous income—revenue that could be channeled into poverty alleviation. Even a fraction of a percent would have made an enormous difference.

After *attac* was founded in France, German activists followed suit, launching *attac Germany*. I attended some of the group's first meetings, where it quickly became clear that we needed a flyer to introduce the concept and attract supporters. I offered to design and fund it. That initial flyer marked the launch of *attac Germany* and generated numerous followers.

For a time, the idea of the Tobin Tax gained real momentum. Even German Finance Minister Wolfgang Schäuble expressed support. But ultimately, the proposal withered. It died a slow and quiet death—pushed aside by more powerful interests.

Still, the broader debate on taxing the super-rich remains alive. Today, there are nearly 3,000 dollar billionaires worldwide—800 of them in the United States alone. Even China counts over 400. According to Oxfam, American billionaires pay less in taxes, proportionally, than most teachers and retail workers.

The numbers are staggering. A 2021 White House study revealed that the 400 wealthiest billionaire families in the U.S. paid an average federal income tax rate of just 8.2 percent. In contrast, the average American taxpayer paid around 13 percent.

Some have floated a more radical solution: to confiscate all wealth exceeding one billion dollars—leaving billionaires with "only" one billion. That's still a thousand million, more than enough to live a life of abundance. But as appealing as such a proposal may sound to some of us, the reality is that these individuals are far too powerful and influential to let this happen.

The debate continues—and rightly so. Economic justice remains a central challenge of our time.

Overall, my attention was never primarily on the wealthy of this world, but rather on the poorest—especially the children. Children who often lack even the most basic of needs: clean water, enough food, access to education, a place to call home, and medical care when illness strikes.

To raise awareness for these children, an artist from Berlin approached us one day with a striking idea: He wanted to light a record-breaking one million candles around the Victory Column in Berlin. The event was to honor the children of the world and raise funds on their behalf. He asked for our cooperation in making this vision a reality—and we agreed without hesitation.

The Victory Column, built in 1873, stands tall in the center of the *Großer Stern* ("Great Star"), a major roundabout in Berlin with a direct view toward the Brandenburg Gate. The artist, Misha Bolourie, was a painter and performance artist originally from Iran. He had long used his art to engage with social themes. A few years earlier, he had drawn attention by lighting 100,000 candles in front of the Cologne Cathedral. But this event in Berlin—"Lichter für Kinder" ("Lights for Kids")—was to be his most ambitious.

Bolourie enlisted the help of Berlin schoolchildren. On August 20, 2004, around 5,000 pupils came together to light one million candles that World Vision and the artist had prepared for the occasion. The wind that evening kept blowing out the flames, and many of the candles had to be relit again and again. Still, the determination of the children didn't waver.

As the dusk deepened, music filled the air—Simon Stockhausen and his ensemble of eight musicians performed a soundscape inspired by cultures from around the world. Slowly, the one million flames flickered to life, transforming the square into a sea of light—a breathtaking sight that moved both the children who lit the candles and the public watching on (Images).

To make the event possible, traffic had to be halted in what is usually one of Berlin's busiest intersections. But the cause justified the pause. For World Vision, the event drew significant public attention. It gave us the opportunity to remind people that 500 million children around the globe were living on less than a dollar a day; that 150 million children were chronically under-nourished; and that at least 100 million children could not yet attend school.

As World Vision's Director of Public Relations, I was responsible for communications surrounding the event. Fortunately, I had excellent staff and specialists assisting me in this effort. And by the time the last candle had flickered out, there was hardly a Berlin citizen left who hadn not heard of World Vision—or the children we work for.

One of my last international trips on behalf of World Vision followed the devastating tsunami that struck Southeast Asia on December 26, 2004. A massive 9.1-magnitude earthquake west of *SUMATRA* unleashed tsunami waves traveling at over 800 kilometers per hour, ravaging coastal regions in more than a dozen countries. With 230,000 lives lost, it became one of the deadliest natural disasters in modern history.

The hardest-hit area was the town of Banda Aceh at the northern tip of Sumatra. Waves up to 30 meters high swept through the city, destroying most of its buildings and killing around 60,000 people. It became the epicenter of unimaginable devastation. Amid the wreckage, only a mosque remained standing—by what many called divine intervention.

In January 2005, I flew to Medan in North Sumatra and from there continued to Banda Aceh. What I saw resembled the aftermath of a nuclear explosion. The city was flattened. Debris was scattered everywhere. Fishing boats had been thrown into the heart of town. Here and there, the bodies of the dead still lay unburied. I was taken along the coast, where the destruction was equally horrifying. Villages had vanished within minutes. Roads, bridges, and farmlands were swept away. The sea had thrown ships onto land and churned entire neighborhoods into rubble. It was the greatest disaster I have ever witnessed.

The tsunami also triggered the largest wave of global donations the world had ever seen. Relief agencies from all over had already arrived in Banda Aceh, many still living in tents, struggling to find shelter and resources. There was a desperate need for coordination, as the situation on the ground remained chaotic.

World Vision had been there from day one—distributing emergency aid, providing temporary shelter, and coordinating relief flights. I was asked to help with food distribution (Image). We also delivered eight ambulances and medical supplies to the local hospital, and planned to set up "child-friendly spaces" to support traumatized children.

Once the immediate emergency phase passed, World Vision would support reconstruction efforts in Banda Aceh and surrounding areas. Today, 20 years after that terrifying tsunami, the city has been fully rebuilt and looks better than ever. But at the time, the grief over the immense loss was everywhere. Amid the despair, however, there were also stories of survival—stories that stayed with me.

One of them was that of Yusni Arni, a 35-year-old widowed mother. She had been feeling ill that morning and was still in bed when the earthquake struck at 7:58 a.m. Terrified, she grabbed her three-year-old daughter Ade and ran into the street, joining neighbors who had also fled their homes. Her two sons, likely playing nearby, were nowhere in sight.

Though her neighborhood had survived the tremor without major damage, people stood confused and shaken—when about fifteen minutes later, they heard what Yusni described as "gunshots."

"The water is coming! The water is coming!" her neighbors shouted.

Cradling her daughter, Yusni ran for higher ground and climbed aboard a truck with others. As the tsunami swept in, the truck was surrounded by water and debris. She feared for her sons—certain they had drowned.

"I felt my life was withering away. All my hopes for the future seemed to fall apart."

Wave after wave crashed down. The city was swallowed by the ocean.

When the worst had passed, others helped her down from the truck. Disoriented, she followed a group of survivors to the mosque.

"There I saw my two boys—alive," she recalled. "I was so overwhelmed I couldn't say a word."

Neighbors had helped Tajalli (8) and Hamid (5) onto a rooftop. Twice the tsunami washed them down. Twice, someone pulled them back up. Yusni's mother survived, too. When asked if she had returned to her house, Yusni said quietly:

"No, I fear to be re-traumatized if I do. And I am afraid of the deadly smell."

When I spoke to her, she lived with her children in a makeshift shack. It wasn't a home—but at least it kept out the rain. She smiled when receiving World Vision's relief package: bottled water, rice, noodles, kitchenware, a hygiene kit, a flashlight. She still lacked sugar and oil, and we promised to help with that, too.

Thanks to her education, Yusni had been selected to help lead one of the new "child-friendly spaces" for children aged 6 to 11. These were safe havens for children to draw, write, and speak about their trauma. There would be space for stories, for laughter, for play—for being a child again.

"I'm glad that World Vision is doing this," Yusni said, "so the kids can learn and play again."

Not everyone had such fortune, however.

I met Sam Siah, a 41-year-old mother of six, at a distribution center in Lam Su Jen. She and her two oldest sons, aged 15 and 11, had tried to flee to higher ground when the wave came. They were caught in the flood, tossed about, struggling to breathe—but they survived.

Her husband and four younger children did not, however. They were never found.

Of her village, Pudeng—just southwest of Banda Aceh—156 survived, and 126 perished.

At the distribution center, she and her boys received food, clothing, mosquito nets, and hygiene kits. The center had space for only 20 people, so most slept outside. Among them were 31 children who had lost at least one parent. Here, too, World Vision was planning to open a child-friendly space—to restore, if only in part, some sense of normalcy.

And then there was Ibrahim.

Eighty years old, frail and thin, he had been sitting outside his house—about a kilometer from the ocean—when he saw the wave approaching. Without hesitation, he climbed a 5-meter-high orange tree in front of his home. The wave hit with full force, bending the tree 45 degrees. His wooden house vanished beneath the water while he clung to the branches just a meter above the surge.

"All I could think of was that I wanted to live," he told us.

And live he did.

Fifteen minutes later, the water receded. He climbed down to find his home gone, replaced by wreckage. He now sat quietly at a school in Lam Su Jen, several kilometers inland, among 220 survivors waiting for food and support. The roads were so badly damaged that aid could only reach them by helicopter.

These were just a few of the stories I was told in northern Sumatra—where the tsunami struck with such brutal force, and where survival often hung by the thinnest thread.

After a few days, it was time for me to return home. I booked a flight to Medan, to be followed by a connecting flight to Kuala Lumpur. Upon arriving in Medan, I was informed that the flight to Kuala Lumpur had been canceled for the day, and I was rebooked on a flight the following day. I was handed a list of hotels and called three of them to check availability. Unfortunately, all the hotels in Medan were fully occupied.

What was I supposed to do in that situation? Spend the night on the street? That wouldn't have been a disaster, given the many tragedies the tsunami had caused. But did I need to?

I decided to call a taxi and instructed the driver to take me to the best hotel in town. He brought me to the Marriott Hotel. After paying the driver and collecting my luggage, I headed to the check-in counter.

"I'd like to check in," I said, giving the impression that I had booked a hotel room.

The receptionist asked, "What's your name, please?"

I gave my name, and she checked the computer.

"I'm sorry," she said. "We don't have a reservation for you. We're fully booked."

"Someone must have made a mistake," I replied. "Maybe you could upgrade me to a suite?"

I knew that most high-end hotels kept a room or a suite in reserve for exceptional situations like this, so I stood my ground, waiting patiently.

After some discussions behind the counter, they didn't offer me a suite, but an ordinary hotel room—which was perfectly fine with me. I couldn't help but smile, feeling pleased with my little maneuver. I had a good night's sleep and was set to fly home early the next morning.

The Final Years

The year 2006 was exceptional for me in several ways.

For one, I turned 60 in July. In many parts of the world, turning 60 holds special significance. In China, for example, it marks the start of a new phase in one's life, the last one: old age – after childhood, teenage years, young adulthood, and adulthood It's a time when people reflect on their accomplishments and on what remains undone. I, too, found myself reflecting on my life. I could look back on an interesting journey so far and wondered what the future still held for me. What was yet to come?

Another reason why 2006 was significant for me, was that it marked ten years of my role as P.R. Director and Spokesperson for World Vision Germany. While I had a great team of co-workers who had supported me over the years, the job was beginning to exhaust me. I felt that someone better equipped than myself should take on the responsibility moving forward. After discussing this with my CEO, we began searching for a replacement.

We also had an idea for what I could do next: We decided to create a small "World Vision Institute for Research and Development," a project I would head. "Development" here wasn't meant to refer to technological advancement, but to poverty alleviation. Once my successor was in place, I transitioned into the role of head of the World Vision Institute and of Research Advisor for World Vision Germany. We produced numerous research papers that documented the invaluable work World Vision was doing.

The third major milestone of 2006 was the publication of my first book. I had long hoped to publish a book and had made several attempts over the years, but it was only at the age of 60 that this long-held goal finally came to fruition. My book, "Der Traum von einer besseren Welt" ("The Dream of a Better World"), was published by a Christian publishing house. In it, I outlined how poverty could be alleviated, especially among children. It was about orphans, street children, child soldiers, child slaves, disabled children, and sexually abused children. But it also addressed more general topics such as emergency relief, development alleviation, providing clean water, basic education, primary health care, and combating HIV/AIDS. Additionally, it discussed issues of peace and reconciliation, with visions of a better world.

On my 60th birthday, I invited friends and family and was proud to hand them a copy of my book. My vision for a better world was one without extreme poverty—a world where human rights are respected everywhere, social justice prevails, and peace and democracy thrive. It was also a world dedicated to preserving the planet and conserving its resources. The book's chapter on "Visions for a Better World" ended with this statement: "A vision without a task is only a dream; a task without a vision is only drudgery; a vision *and* a task is the hope of the world." One young reader later wrote to me, saying, "I want your vision to become mine, too." This young girl went on to spend many years working in poverty alleviation. Following the book's release, it became required reading for all new staff at World Vision Germany.

The fourth reason why 2006 was so special was an unfortunate one—it marked a period of severe crisis in my relationship with Aline. From the very beginning, we had struggled with emotional issues, with many hours of discussion, but rarely any resolution. Over time, the situation deteriorated, and doubts about the future of our relationship grew on both sides. Ultimately, this led to our virtual separation in 2007.

The reasons behind the separation were complex, shared between both of us. I had long struggled with Aline's emotionality, and I had my own emotional challenges to deal with as well. Moments of my own disloyalty compounded these problems. On several occations, we both sought help from psychotherapists. But in the end, we decided to part ways.

Since our separation, I have made efforts to maintain a cordial, friendly connection with Aline. At times, this has worked, but at others, it has proven difficult. As I write this, we are still trying to navigate a way of relating to each other that honors our shared history and the individuals we have become. The journey is ongoing, with no clear resolution in sight. Life is a mixture of happiness and disappointment, of highlights and regrets. I have remained single ever since, unable or unwilling to enter into another long-term relationship – partly because I was not prepared to once again invest my emotions and sacrifice my way of life, partly out of respect for Aline whom I continue to honor and appreciate for what she was and still is.

After our separation, I threw myself into hard work, determined not to succumb to self-pity. For several months, I managed to keep my emotions in check—until a severe flu struck, forcing me to stay home for several days. By the third day, I suddenly experienced what I can only describe as a panic attack. A deep, gut-wrenching fear gripped me—the terror of having to live alone from now on and not being able to cope with it. I couldn't bear the thought of being awake, yet I couldn't sleep either. My anxiety was so overwhelming that I called Aline the next day, as well as my brother, both of whom offered and provided their willing assistance. Their support helped me survive that week, and I emerged from the experience sound and safe, though shaken.

However, it became clear to me that I needed to talk about all the emotional disturbances I was grappling with. So, I decided to start a men's group. Drawing on my past experiences with group therapy, I hoped that this would offer some respite from the emotional turmoil I was facing. In the end, some five or six men joined my group, and we met weekly to share our respective struggles and relational predicaments. Over the course of four years, the group became a lifeline for most of us, a space where we could speak openly and honestly about our emotional challenges and find solace in each other's experiences.

Even before our separation – and in light of my upcoming retirement –, I had already sensed the need to find a new focus, a way to compensate for the emotional void. I turned again to writing, having published my first book already, albeit at an advanced age.

I published several additional books, some of which had to do with World Vision. One was *Janet and the Grey Death* (2007), which focused on the plight of children living in a world ravaged by HIV/AIDS. In 2008, I published an anthology about *HIV and AIDS as a Christian Challenge*, in which the moral and theological implications of this epidemic were examined by several authors. In 2010, I was asked to write a book on *Child Poverty*, which looked at the state of children in need both in my home country and around the globe. In 2011, I published another anthology (*Handbuch Spendenwesen*, 2011), a handbook covering the organization, transparency, control, and financial management of non-profit organizations.

But I also wanted to cover topics having to do with my understanding of the world and of theology. After all, I had spent years in trying to reconcile religion with the natural sciences. I first thought about a book addressing the relationship between theology and science. But as it turned out, I wrote a book on theology and another one on my world view.

The theological book I wrote has the title *The Reality of God: How We Can Believe in God in the 21st Century* (2012/2015). It offers a variety of perspectives on the concept of God, and it was well-received by a number of theologians, sparking thoughtful discussions on the topic.

My next work focused on the world itself (2015). The German title was *Und sie dreht sich doch!* (*"And Yet It Moves"*), with the telling subtitle, *50 Answers to the Question of How Everything Began*. The book was divided into two main sections. The first explored mythologies surrounding the origin of the world, while the second delved into the modern cosmological worldview as presented by astrophysicists. I had spent much time learning about astrophysics and cosmology, and this expertise was incorporated into that book. It ended with an interesting chapter on the origin of life, and of consciousness, and why there is anything at all, rather than nothing. The book was well received, with one prominent church leader recommending that every pastor should read it.

But there was more to come …

Already in 2005, I had read about a book entitled *The Hidden Origins of Islam* (*Die dunklen Anfänge*, 2005), which I promptly purchased and read with great interest. The book signaled to me that serious attempts were being made by some Orientalists and scholars of Islam to approach the Quran and Islam from a strictly historical-critical perspective.

Among the book's thought-provoking chapters was an important piece by Christoph Luxenberg on the Dome of the Rock in Jerusalem and its inscriptions. Luxenberg's analysis revealed that the inscriptions inside the Dome, commissioned by the Umayyad Caliph Abd al-Malik in the late 7th century, indicated a very specific view of Jesus and his nature. The caliph denied the divinity of Jesus, asserting that he should neither be called "the Son of God" nor as "God," for there could be but one God and one God alone. However, the inscriptions referred to Jesus as "the Son of Mary," "the Messenger," "the

Prophet," "the Word" (Logos), "God's Servant," "the Christ," and "the Word of Truth." The whole inscription is about Jesus.

More startling still, the name "Muhammad" (MHMD) appeared in the inscription, reading: "MHMD is the Servant of God and His Messenger. God and His angels bless the Prophet." The four-letter word "MHMD" could either be understood as a participle ("Praised be the Servant of God"—referring to Jesus), or as an epithet ("The Praised One is the Servant of God"), or as a proper name ("Muhammad is the Servant of God").

Luxenberg contended that "MHMD" should be interpreted here as a participle. Other scholars, however, debated whether it should be taken as a mutated epithet or, in a more conventional reading, as the name of the Arab prophet. The problem regarding the latter was that the entire inscription was obviously about Jesus, while the Arab prophet was nowhere in the Dome introduced or described (other than that his name seemed to appear).

Upon reading this article, I was stunned, to say the least. If "MHMD" indeed referred to Jesus, as the inscription suggested, then the entire traditional narrative of Muhammad's origins and the formation of Islam would be called into question. That conclusion, I thought, was too revolutionary to be accepted without further scrutiny. Either Luxenberg was correct, and further research would have to confirm his theory, or he was mistaken, and further investigation would disprove him.

In order to verify or falsify Luxenberg's interpretation, I realized one would need to explore modern scholarship on several crucial topics: on the Quran, on the Muslim Hadith tradition, on the Sira (the biography of Muhammad by Ibn Ishaq), and on other contemporary evidence. But this undertaking appeared Herculean to me. Was I prepared to tackle it? I decided the task was both timely and urgent, and I set out to confront this challenge.

Over the next five years, I meticulously reviewed countless publications on these topics. I began with some preliminaries. Since this was going to be a historical as well as a religious study, I first asked the questions of what *history* was all about and how to understand *religion*.

But the core of my research focused on the Hadith, the Sira, and the Qur'an. I learned that the *Hadith* tradition in many ways holds more influence over Muslims than the Quran itself. Besides, the vast majority of hadiths were written too late to be considered reliable sources for the period they purport to document. Even the medieval Muslims knew that most hadiths were invented, and they sought to devise methods to separate the wheat from the chaff. But even many of the alleged "authentic hadiths" appeared to me as being farfetched, improbable, and unhistorical.

I then turned my attention to the scholarship surrounding the *Sira* of Ibn Ishaq, which forms the backbone of the conventional narrative of Islam's origins. Not only was the Sira written long after the events it describes, but it also relied heavily on unreliable hadiths. From the perspective of a modern historian, the Sira can hardly qualify as a sound historical source.

Next, I examined the modern scholarship on the Quran itself; and what I uncovered was a confusing and fragmented field of research. There was little conclusive evidence to support the traditional narrative of the Quran's authorship by an Arab prophet named Muhammad. The canonical story of the Quran's origin seemed primarily based on dubious hadiths and questionable Quranic interpretations (known as *tafsir* in Arabic).

Finally, I reviewed Orientalist scholarship on contemporary evidence, such as 7th-century inscriptions (apart from those in the Dome of the Rock). Did these inscriptions support or challenge the traditional narrative?

The results of my inquiries were both enlightening and sobering: Much of the conventional narrative appeared to be grounded in unreliable sources—many of them written centuries after the events they claimed to report about. While I cannot go into exhaustive detail here, suffice it to say that all my research appeared to confirm Luxenberg's thesis: The term "Muhammad" (MHMD) in the Dome of the Rock inscriptions ought to be understood as referring to Jesus, the Son of Mary. And subsequent references to "Muhammad" on coins and other documents could and should be viewed in that context.

It appeared that, over time, the figure of Muhammad evolved and was transformed, and the name became increasingly associated with an *Arab* prophet, becoming tightly interwoven with Arab history and identity. As a result, a good number of scholars now question the historicity of the Arab prophet as a figure distinct from the person mentioned in the early inscriptions.

Christoph Luxenberg – a pseudonym – had not only written the article on the Dome of the Rock that piqued my interest in the early history of Islam, but he had also authored a groundbreaking book on the Quran, entitled *The Syro-Aramaic Reading of the Koran*. In this work, he showed that much of the Quran could only be fully understood by considering its potential roots in Aramaic texts or oral traditions.

My exhaustive research culminated in what may be my *magnum opus*, a 900-page study in small print, with an additional 40 pages of bibliography. Published in 2016 by the esteemed Springer Publishing House, *Muhammad: A Historical-Critical Study on the Origins of Islam and Its Prophet* has since become a German reference work for anyone seeking a thorough understanding of early Islamic history. But while it is found in major university libraries, it has not received the full appreciation it deserves, I think, within the academic community—mostly because its conclusions are so revolutionary. And also, because I was not an established Orientalist. One reviewer, however, commented on my work with the words: "Bangert has sifted through a monumental body of material and composed a comprehensive overview that is unparalleled in both the German-speaking and international realms; he has produced a fair, balanced, and carefully worded text."

In 2018, I took each of the major chapters of that comprehensive book and transformed them into six smaller volumes, which I published in my own small private publishing company *Philia Verlag*. For many non-academic readers, these more accessible books serve as an engaging introduction to the subject.

To properly engage with the research sources—particularly with the Arab and Aramaic scripts—I needed at least a basic understanding of both languages. I took courses in Arabic, which were readily available in Germany. But to learn Aramaic, the language of Jesus, I spent my 2009 vacation at the St. Ephrem Ecumenical Research Institute (SEERI) in **KOTTAYAM, INDIA**. This institute in southwest India is the only one for advanced teaching and learning of the Syriac-Aramaic language and heritage. This trip turned out to be my final journey to India, a country that had shaped many earlier stages of my life and work.

In my new role as the head of the World Vision Institute, I also undertook a good number of international trips to participate in conferences and to give talks on various subjects. One conference was the 15th UN Climate Change Conference in Copenhagen (December 2009). Several other conferences were held in Vienna. These included the Liechtenstein Colloquium in June 2009 where I spoke on "Religion, Development and the Global Financial Crisis;" then an NGO meeting prior to the World AIDS Conference in Vienna in August 2009, where I spoke about "HIV and AIDS as a Theological Problem;" and an International Conference on Poverty and Social Exclusion in October 2010, where I spoke on "Europe's Responsibility for the World's Absolute Poor." I cannot list here all the conferences I attended or the lectures I gave.

In 2011, I officially retired. However, I continued working half-time for another year and a half, in agreement with World Vision Germany. As I had become somewhat of a workaholic, I was grateful for this time of transition. After that period, I retired fully from professional employment. Still, I remained active in civil society: For four years, I served on the board of an umbrella organization for development NGOs in the state of Hesse, and I also continued as chair of the Board of Arbitration for the German umbrella organization VENRO, a position I held until 2023.

In 2017, I was invited by the German watchdog agency DZI to provide training in nonprofit governance in **PRAGUE**. Civil society actors in the Czech Republic were intent on establishing a watchdog institution for their own country and needed more background information on how to evaluate nonprofit organizations in areas such as organizational structure, transparency, financial accountability, and public communication. I gladly held that workshop in Prague; and with the honorarium I received for it, I took the opportunity to travel to Morocco—a long-held dream. It was a journey without any purpose or function – other than personal enjoyment.

In **MAROCCO**, I visited Fes, Casablanca, Essaouira, Rabat, and Marrakesh. The city of Marrakesh struck me as the very embodiment of the Maghreb society, a living tapestry of color and chaos, of scents and sounds that dazzled the senses. The labyrinthine souks pulsed with life, every corner revealing stalls brimming with exotic spices, fragrant teas, gleaming lanterns, and handcrafted treasures. In these bustling alleys, where negotiation is an art and storytelling a currency, I haggled with merchants and marveled at their wares—colorful lamps, ornate silverwork, and time-worn teapots that seemed to whisper of centuries past. It was a fitting culmination of years of engagement with the Arab world, not through books alone, but through lived experience (Images).

In early 2018, my son Patrick informed me that he and his partner were planning to marry on August 11 of that year. He asked if I would be willing to officiate a small, family-limited wedding ceremony. Naturally, I was honored and gladly agreed.

As for Patrick and his bride-to-be, Famida, they had first met exactly 25 years earlier, back in 1993, when both were students at the International School of Manila (cf. p. 142 of this book). Famida came from a Bangladeshi Muslim family, but had attended a Catholic school and was religiously open-minded. Her father was working for an international bank in the Philippines at the time. A bond had quickly formed between the two teenagers. However, when her parents discovered the relationship, they disapproved, not least because Patrick was not a Muslim. Despite this intervention, the two young people continued to see each other for some time.

But eventually, life took them down different paths. Famida moved to the United States to study at a women's college, and Patrick relocated to London to pursue mathematics at the University College London. In time, Famida married a Bangladeshi Muslim and had two children, while Patrick completed his Ph.D., became a lecturer at the International University of Bremen, and entered into a long-term relationship of his own. Yet both their relationships ended in separation.

Throughout the years, Patrick and Famida had remained in occasional contact. After their respective breakups, Patrick proposed a bold yet heartfelt idea: "Why not try again?" They did just that. Patrick moved to San Francisco, where Famida lived, and this time, her family raised no objections to their union. Patrick and Famida decided to get officially married exactly 25 years after first having met in Manila.

The wedding was to take place in an elegant restaurant overlooking the shimmering expanse of San Francisco Bay. Famida's extended family, including her once-hesitant parents, attended, as did my wife Aline and I, who had travelled there together for the occasion.

A day before the wedding was to take place, Famida asked me: "Where do you think God is? Is He up there (she pointed to the sky), or is He in here (she pointed to her heart)? Without hesitation, I answered: "He is here in our hearts." She seemed satisfied with that answer. And this was not the time for any theological deliberations.

Patrick's spiritual path had long diverged from mine, for I had never attempted to impose my beliefs on him. Not only had I been in the midst of my own theological reorientation, but I also held the conviction that faith should be an entirely personal matter. While growing up in Penang, Patrick took up Taekwondo and through his trainer was gradually drawn to Buddhism. He admired the fact that Buddhism does not rest on belief in a creator god, but instead offers a structured path toward inner growth and personal maturity. Regular meditation became part of his life and shaped his character. He grew into a calm, reflective individual, someone who listens deeply and in whose company others felt genuinely respected.

Hence, when it came time for me to plan the wedding ceremony, I was faced with an interesting interreligious challenge: the groom was a Buddhist, the bride and her family were Muslims, and I, the officiant, was a Christian theologian. The wedding ceremony itself turned out to be as unique as the couple's journey. I saw this as an opportunity to create a symbolic and inclusive ritual that honored all three traditions. For example, I invited Famida's father to recite the opening chapter of the Quran, the *Fatiha*. The ceremony thus became a gentle convergence of faiths—an expression of mutual respect and shared joy. Everyone seemed pleased with the outcome, and we all sat down afterward to a wonderful celebratory dinner (Images).

It was a beautiful, harmonious occasion, and as it turned out, it was my last journey to the United States—at least thus far.

Beyond that particular voyage, I felt little urge to travel again—having already wandered across so many continents, countries, and cultures of the world. I had set foot on five continents, explored close to 100 countries – some multiple times –, lived among Americans, Africans, and Asians, and formed friendships with people of richly diverse backgrounds. I had tasted the flavors of distant lands, listened to stories shaped by different fates and fortunes, and been profoundly enriched by the experiences each culture offered.

There were only a few more private trips I took. One was to Turkey together with Patrick (Image: Kurt in Pamukkale); another was to the Czech Republic with Aline (Image: Marienbad); and in 2023 I embarked on a solo journey to the timeless beauty of the Dolomites (Image) and the poetic splendor of Venice (Image). My next tour – surely one of the very last – will take me to Poland, Lithuania, Latvia, Estonia, Finland, Sweden and Denmark.

As for my *theological journey*, I had found myself increasingly ideologically "homeless." In 1990, I had joined the Lutheran Church, leaving the Seventh-day Adventist Church behind. While the Lutheran tradition was considerably more liberal than the church I had left, it remained somewhat alien to me, as I had not been socialized within its liturgy, customs, or hierarchy. For a time, I was a "displaced person" in the world of Christian thought—liberal in mindset, yet without a clear community to call my own.

That changed in 2010 when I attended the annual conference of the *Bund für Freies Christentum* (Association for Liberal Christianity) which took place in Arnoldshain, not far from where I lived. I could immediately resonate with their positions and perspectives. Their liberal approach to theology offered a home for my long-evolving views, and I decided to become a member of the association. Three years later, they looked for a new editor of the association's bimonthly journal, *Freies Christentum*, and I was chosen. The role has been deeply rewarding, allowing me to re-engage with theology— this time from an explicitly liberal vantage point.

This might be a good moment to say a few words about "liberal theology" itself. The term is typically associated with a group of German theologians from the 19th and early 20th centuries—figures such as Friedrich Schleiermacher, Ferdinand Christian Baur, Albrecht Ritschl, Adolf von Harnack, Ernst Troeltsch, Wilhelm Herrmann, Martin Rade, and others. Inspired by the Enlightenment, these thinkers adopted a historical-critical approach to the Bible, placed significant emphasis on church history, critically examined traditional dogmas, and sought to reconcile Christianity with the burgeoning modern worldview—particularly the scientific discoveries of their time in biology, geology, and astronomy.

Though rich in historical awareness, these early liberal theologians tended to underemphasize the systematic dimension of theology. In other words,

while they were adept at questioning traditional doctrines, they did not always propose fully reimagined theological systems in their place. This gap opened the door for critique, most notably from the Swiss theologian Karl Barth who contended that theology should not be confined to historical inquiry alone, but must provide a solid foundation for the proclamation of the Gospel. For Barth, the task of theology was to furnish pastors with the tools necessary to preach Christ's message meaningfully in the contemporary world.

Several theologians of the 20th century took Barth's challenge seriously and adapted liberal theology accordingly. Among them, Ulrich Neuenschwander, Paul Tillich, and Dietrich Bonhoeffer stand out. Each in their own way retained the liberal spirit while integrating deeper philosophical and theological reflection and a greater emphasis on systematics.

Following the Second World War, many of Barth's more conservative followers came to shape the dominant contours of German theology that would characterize the next generation of German pastors. On the other hand, a small group of committed liberal thinkers founded the *Bund für Freies Christentum* in 1948, determined to preserve and promote an outright liberal interpretation of the Christian faith. Central to their vision was a departure from some traditional Christological claims—such as the divinity of Christ or his vicarious sacrifice for the world's redemption. These thinkers also proposed a reimagined concept of God—not as an extant "being" residing somewhere beyond the clouds, but as the unfathomable ground of all existence. Their commitment to a historical-critical reading of Scripture also opened the door to accepting the findings of the natural sciences—whether the theory of evolution or cosmological theories of the universe's origin.

Sometimes I am being asked: "If you relativize Christian dogmas, what then remains of the Christian message?" My answer is simple and clear: We are then compelled to return to the message Jesus himself had preached. To center our faith once more on the proclamation of the *Kingdom of God*—the very heart of Jesus' ministry—is to discover a treasure trove of ethical, spiritual, and theological insight. His message remains an inexhaustible source for reflection and action. If we, as Christians, live and embody the Gospel which Jesus preached, then we are his true disciples. *And that Gospel is fundamentally concerned with the healing of individuals and the well-being of society as a whole!*

While researching for my book on the origin of Islam, I had for some time entertained the idea of turning this research into a dissertation, and in fact had made contact to a professor at the university of Halle/Saale, who had been recommended to me; but Halle was quite a distance from where I lived, and I never established a good relationship with that professor. I also contacted two other professors regarding this possibility. For one, my *Mu-*

hammad-book was too lenghty, and for the second, it was too revolutionary. So I gave up on the idea of turning that research into a doctoral dissertation, comforting myself with the fact that our son Patrick had become a Doctor of Mathematics – at the age of 25. Sometimes, we have to wait for our kids to fulfill the dreams we ourselves have not been able to achieve.

In 2019, however, having turned 73, my longtime friend Wolfgang Alberth—who had been my best man at my own wedding—offered an unexpected but intriguing suggestion: "Why not pursue your doctoral degree after all?" Wolfgang, an engineer by profession, had himself studied history of art after his retirement and finished his studies with a dissertation.

At first, I hesitated. It seemed a daunting endeavor at my age. But the more I thought about it, the more I warmed to the idea once again. I decided to explore whether I would meet the necessary prerequisites and, crucially, whether I could find the right supervisor for such an undertaking.

The year before, I had attended a conference on Liberal Theology at the University of Munich. Two speakers in particular made a lasting impression on me: Professor Gary Dorrien of Union Theological Seminary in New York, who spoke eloquently about Alfred North Whitehead; and Professor Claus-Dieter Osthövener from the University of Marburg, who delivered a compelling presentation on the theologian Rudolf Otto. Both of these scholars were deeply insightful and excellent communicators.

After Dorrien's lecture, I approached him to express my interest in his impressive trilogy on American Liberal Theology. He suggested I write to him, and in response to my email, he generously sent me three of his substantial works. I reciprocated by sending him several of my own publications. Through Dorrien's books, I developed a particular appreciation for Walter Rauschenbusch and the powerful vision of the *Social Gospel* that this German-American had championed more than a century ago.

Inspired by Osthövener's lecture and his academic proximity to Rudolf Otto, who had also taught in Marburg more than a century ago, I decided to reach out to him with the idea he might supervise my dissertation. To my delight, he agreed. I initially proposed to focus on Rauschenbusch and the Social Gospel. In response, Osthövener suggested enriching the project with a comparative perspective by also examining the German theologian Martin Rade alongside Rauschenbusch. Rade, another liberal thinker from Marburg, had edited the influential theological magazine *Die Christliche Welt* for nearly four decades before it was terminated during World War II. Osthövener and I agreed that the "social question"—*die soziale Frage*—would serve as the *tertium comparationis* for both theologians.

Later that year, the COVID-19 pandemic emerged and, paradoxically, offered me a unique opportunity: for with much of the world slowing down and most of us staying home, I was able to fully immerse myself in my research. I acquired countless books and borrowed many others from the university libraries in Frankfurt/Main and Marburg, including the entire series of *Die Christliche Welt*. I read virtually all of Rade's articles, many of them devotional pieces written during times of significant societal transformation.

Interestingly, after *Die Christliche Welt* ceased publication during the war, the newly-founded magazine *Freies Christentum*—which I now edit—took up the mantle of liberal theology in 1948. In a sense, I felt as though I had become Martin Rade's successor, albeit more than seventy years after his death.

While conducting research for my dissertation, I also completed another project I had been working on: my book *Gott im liberalen Christentum* ("God in Liberal Christianity"). Here I explored the doctrine of God as it was developed by major thinkers over the past 500 years, from Martin Luther and Giordano Bruno via Kant, Hegel and Schleiermacher to more recent theologians such as Tillich, Bonhoeffer and Dorothee Sölle. I covered almost 50 philosophers and theologians in this book, highlighting the diversity and evolution of theological perspectives across time. I also included a chapter on American liberal theologians such as Alfred North Whitehead, Walter Rauschenbusch, and even Gary Dorrien. The book of 462 pages, published in 2022 by Springer, offers a comprehensive overview of how the concept of God has transformed through the last five centuries.

Nevertheless, my central focus remained on my dissertation (Image). The subject was intriguing to me. Both Rauschenbusch and Rade (Images) lived during the high tide of industrialization, a time when economic upheaval was tearing at the social fabric on both sides of the Atlantic. In the United States, the prevailing ethos favored *laissez-faire* capitalism, with its near-complete trust in the self-regulating power of the free market. In contrast, German society looked more to the state for intervention and social reform. Both theologians, however, felt their churches were neglecting their prophetic role

and needed to address the deepening social inequalities, the vulnerability of the working class, and the erosion of community solidarity.

In Germany, Chancellor Otto von Bismarck had, to his credit, already introduced groundbreaking social insurance systems aimed at protecting workers from illness, unemployment, workplace accidents, and the challenges of old age. The United States, however, remained slow to act. Rauschenbusch and Rade warned of the growing alienation of industrial workers—many of whom had already turned their backs on the church and were increasingly drawn to socialism or even communism. While both theologians acknowledged the appeal of socialist ideals, they rejected the atheism embedded in much of its ideology. They envisioned a third path—a socially committed Christianity that would meet the spiritual and material needs of a changing world.

Tragically, Rauschenbusch's *Social Gospel* lost momentum in the wake of the First World War. Some of its principles were later resurrected by Franklin D. Roosevelt during the New Deal era. In Germany, social legislation persisted half-heartedly until it blossomed after the Second World War in what would become known as the *Soziale Marktwirtschaft*—the social market economy.

I not only compared the two theologians and their respective economic environments, but I also included a chapter about the current state of affairs in both countries. I also asked what we could learn from these two pioneers when looking at today's social inequalities in the United States and Germany. I completed my dissertation in late 2023.

In April 2024, I defended my study in a formal *disputatio*, and when it was published—again by Springer—in November of that year, I officially became a Doctor of Theology at the age of 78! It was a satisfying milestone, the realization of a long-held aspiration. It was only now that I informed family and friends about it, who commended me on this late achievement. I even got an appreciative note from a person I had long forgotten. In 1999, when travelling by ferry from Italy to Albania, I had met Gamend Cikaci, a young Kosovar who gave me valuable information regarding Albania and Kosovo. 25 years later, I suddenly received a message from him just to commend me on my doctorate. He had accidentally found out about it in the internet.

In 2025, my dissertation was published in English. In the same year, I also prepared an abbreviated English version of "Muhammad and the Origin of Islam," to be printed in 2026. And I finally also published a book that I had been wanting to write since studying theology in Tübingen: a book on the historical-critical interpretation of the Bible. It, too, was printed in 2026. During this time, I also wrote this autobiography.

Looking back upon my life, I realize just how varied and colorful my *professional journey* has been. I first trained as a compositor and layout designer, then—with CBM—got involved in the rehabilitation of the blind and disabled and the prevention of blindness. Working for World Vision, I became a public relations director, an advocate for poverty alleviation, and a nonprofit governance specialist. Rather late in life, I became an expert of comparative religion with a special focus on early Islam. And now, at last, I stand also as an accomplished theologian—with a special expertise on the question of God, on social ethics, and on the question of hermeneutics.

At this point, I must say something about the quiet rewards of friendship. Wolfgang Alberth, whom I had known since my days in Tübingen was more than a friend. He not only encouraged me to embrace this latest challenge of a doctoral dissertation, but he also encouraged me throughout my research. I wonder whether I would have completed that task without his unwavering support. He certainly was (and still is) a steadfast companion on my journey.

There have been other individuals whose friendship I have cherished over the years:

There was Ted Mamoulelis—my Greek fellow student, whom I met in Tennessee and who persuaded me to come to California. He once came to visit me in Germany, and I also visited him once when he lived in Sacramento. His life was cut far too short, yet his presence remains a bright thread in my memories.

Then there is Rudi Maier, my companion in theology at Pacific Union College and at Andrews University. He tended our lifelong friendship with unwavering faithfulness—a quiet constancy I deeply treasure. He now lives in Tennessee, where I started my American journey.

Bernd Rieckhof must also be mentioned. We studied theology together at Andrews University before he turned to pharmacy and medicine. Our minds met in the realm of liberal thought, and to this day, we enjoy an occasional, meaningful exchange—each one a reaffirmation of our close connection.

Then, of course, there is Peter Gergel who came to Germany from Transylvania and was my valued colleague at the Christian Blind Mission (CBM). Our friendship has lasted now for more than 40 years. We still see each other quite frequently and enjoy each others company.

Jürgen Unger, a successful architect, entered my life through the Freemason Lodge in Friedberg. We spent countless evenings together—often with his wife, Karin—sharing conversation, ideas, and laughter. He was a friend precisely because he was so different from me. I spoke at his funeral in 2024. May he rest in peace.

And last, but certainly not least, I must mention the late Helmut Fischer—once professor at the Theological Seminary in Friedberg. A kindred liberal spirit, he was a brilliant thinker, a gifted orator, and the author of numerous theological works—a few of which I had the privilege to help publish. Living nearby in Bad Nauheim, he became a cherished friend (Image). We spent many afternoons and evenings lost in conversation, exploring the depths of philosophy and theology. Especially when we disagreed, our discussions sparked new insights—rich, rewarding dialogues that were often joined and enjoyed by his dear wife, Ursula. I will always remember them.

These friendships, each unique, have helped to shape the contours of my life. And I carry them with me still—with gratitude, reverence, and joy.

In January 2024, I received an invitation from a number of liberally-minded Christian groups to attend a meeting at the University of Göttingen. The purpose of the gathering was to reflect on the pressing need for church reform—a topic that had gained significant urgency in recent years, particularly in light of many Europeans leaving the churches and also because of numerous child abuse cases – primarily, but not exclusively, within the Catholic Church. Beyond that, however, there was a broader and deeper sense that the institutional churches had failed to adequately respond to a changing world—one in which traditional dogmas were increasingly challenged by historical-critical methods and modern insights into human nature, ethics, and spirituality.

It was both refreshing and encouraging to find myself among more than twenty academics (mostly theologians) who shared similar convictions. We were a diverse but like-minded group, unified by our desire to see the Christian message renewed and made relevant for today's world. As a result of our discussions, we founded a new network (*"Netzwerk Christsein heute"*) committed to advancing bold, radical church reforms. We also drafted and adopted the *Göttinger Manifest 2024*, a statement that laid out our vision for what such a reform should entail.

The *Netzwerk* made clear that Christianity should not be defined by rigid doctrinal affirmations, but rather by its service to people—their needs, their dignity, and their well-bing. It called for a return to the Gospel message of the *Kingdom of God*, as Jesus himself had preached it: not a future paradise in a distant realm, but a vision of human and societal wholeness, grounded in justice, compassion, and spiritual vitality. The Kingdom of God, in Jesus' proclamation, was about healing the broken, uplifting the marginalized, and fostering communities rooted in love and mutual support.

183

Crucially, the *Netzwerk* also urged a rethinking of our understanding of God. Instead of conceiving of God as a distinct, remote being in the heavens—*sui generis* and detached from the world—we propose an image of God as the depth of being, the ground of all existence, the transformative power embedded in reality itself. In this way, the divine becomes not an object of belief but a source of renewal, growth, and meaning.

I was honored to be selected to the editorial group that formulated the *Göttinger Manifest*, and was also elected to the leadership team of the *Netzwerk*. Whether this network will have a tangible impact on the churches remains to be seen. Institutional religion has often been slow—painfully slow—to embrace change, and that pattern may well continue. But at the very least, we created a space, a haven, for those who share a liberal understanding of Christianity—a space for mutual encouragement, theological reflection, and spiritual community.

In Germany, at least, the urgency for reform is hard to ignore. The exodus from the mainstream churches continues at an alarming pace. Increasingly, people feel disconnected from institutional religion, which many perceive as outdated, moralistic, or irrelevant to their lives. There is even a growing sentiment that religion itself may no longer be necessary in a modern, secular world.

I personally believe that this stance is a profound mistake. For in my view, every human being is, at heart, a *homo religiosus*—a being inherently in need of, and oriented toward, meaning, depth, and transcendence. Sooner or later, each person must face the spiritual dimension of his or her life, whether through joy, crisis, loss, or wonder. Life is far more than material success or economic achievement. True well-being encompasses not only physical health and material well-being, but also emotional resilience, social connection, and, last but not least, spiritual depth.

An holistic, contemporary Christianity must speak to all these aspects of human life. It must move beyond dogma and formality, and become once again a transformative force—personal and societal, inner and outer. That, I believe, is the challenge and the hope of our time.